Don't Waste Money, Spend it!

Don't Waste Money, Spend it!

Come Join Renowned Tightwad Lisa Wysocki in Her Madcap Adventures in Thriftiness and Frugality

by Lisa Wysocki

iUniverse, Inc.

New York Lincoln Shanghai

Don't Waste Money, Spend it!

iUniverse, Inc.

For information address:
iUniverse, Inc.
2021 Pine Lake Road, Suite 100
Lincoln, NE 68512
www.iuniverse.com

ISBN: 0-595-31292-6

Dedicated to my father and to Dollface
(who has been lobbying for a dedication and deserves it).

Benjamin Franklin chose 13 virtues he would strive to achieve. Number 5 was Frugality. On frugality he wrote, "Make no expence (sic) but to do good to others or yourself; i.e. waste nothing."

Contents

1

Disclaimer Or Oh The Folly Of Wasted Money

First of all, I want to make this disclaimer for those who might read this and think I am a smarty-pants or insufferable know-it-all. Rest assured there are many things I am truly bad at. I could not decorate a closet if I was locked in it with decorating books for days. My voice is as nasal and abrasive as you can imagine, and I cannot come close to carrying a tune. I am an awful athlete and am grateful that my fabulous exercise class still lets me in with my distracting, lousy form.

I could go on and on. My French accent is so offensive that when I was in France they begged me to speak English. I cannot knit, sew, crochet or needle-point. In addition, I am a sorry bridge player and my six year old is starting to beat me in Chess. I am untalented as a gardener and fret whenever someone gives me a plant to take care of. I prefer cut flowers that are already pre-destined to die within a week.

I was lucky to have found at least one area that I can excel in and that is, frugality. What do I mean by frugality? The *Webster's Dictionary* defines frugality as "characterized by or reflecting economy in the expenditure of resources". However, I would like to submit to you my own personal and up-to-date version. To me, frugality means the "non-wasting" of money. I have nothing against spending money (reasonably), but I am vehemently opposed to wasting it.

In this book I will reveal the rules of spending money so you can avoid the trap of needlessly wasting it. By following my practical tips you can challenge the old adage that you cannot spend it twice. Sometimes you can in fact, spent it twice. If you regrettably waste it, I will show you how you can get a second chance to spend it again. I will share my ideas on how to recover lost money. We will refer to this skill as the art of rescuing your money.

You may ask what are my credentials to be the giver of financial advice, especially in light of all my shortcomings. I have a Masters in Organizational Psychol-

1

ogy from Columbia University and a Masters in Business Administration from Fordham University (all paid for by a former employer's tuition reimbursement program). In addition, I have two Bachelors Degrees from Carnegie Mellon University, one in Economics and one in Administration and Management Science.

But just because you are a well educated person does not automatically make you a good money manager. In my case, I was able to use my background in business and psychology and apply it to my personal money matters. My goal is to share my strategies with you and help you to get started on the same path that I am on, the path that leads towards financial freedom.

Being Stupid And Foolish Is Not Cheap!

But before we begin this adventure and before I begin dispensing valuable and practical advice, I need to get a few things off my chest and purge. I want to share my personal stories of how I wasted money. These are the wasteful follies that still continue to haunt me. Think of this as a kind of twelve step program where you first need to "fess-up" to all your past transgressions.

I invite you now to laugh with me as I tell you about some of my past follies. You may marvel about how someone like me with good financial sense could act like such a nincompoop. But, even the mighty practitioners of frugality may fall. I have made some ridiculous spending mistakes that I will now share with you. Some of these incidents still confound me to this day. How could I have been so dimwitted?

For starters there was the time I was on the Disney Cruise with my mother and my little boy Matthew. I called my husband to check on the pets. In retrospect he made a huge blunder by confessing to me that Pepper the cat had been missing for over 24 hours. He probably should have kept that to himself and not send me "overboard" on the cruise. I proceeded to fight with my husband ship to shore over Pepper's whereabouts. The good news is that Pepper returned home late that night.

I was thrilled that my little kitty was safe, but soon after the bad news hit when I received my bill. My eyes were instantly drawn to a line item on my bill for over $300.00 for phone calls. Who knew that ship to shore was so expensive? Now I am more likely to have a fight over email.

Then there was the catastrophic blunder when I did not do my due diligence and hired a plumber to fix a $50,000 plumbing problem (more to follow on that). Or when I paid to have light bulbs fixed on my cars that were covered under warranty (ouch!). Once I even took $50.00 out of an ATM only to be in such a hurry that I left without the cash. Believe it or not I went back for it about 15 minutes later and it was still there (as thrilling as it was to see my money hanging out and waiting for me, I do not recommend that you try this on your own!)

And sometimes when I thought I was being frugal I was just being foolish. By being young, cheap and naive I got myself into a real can of worms in Italy. I was backpacking through Europe as a disciple of *Arthur Frommer's Europe on $10.00 a Day.* I was in Italy and thought I figured out that I did not really need to pay the bus fare as I toured Rome. It was the honor system and unfortunately I was not behaving very honorably.

What I did not anticipate was a spontaneous spot check by the Italian police. I really thought the Italians were too chaotic to check on anything, silly me! When the authorities boarded the bus I spent a few minutes picking up used tickets from the floor and handing them over hoping that one was a legitimate ticket. This became less amusing after the first dozen or so of duds.

Finally, the police attempted to escort me off the bus to have me arrested. If not for the Italians who were taken in by my flood of tears (I am sure I looked like a pathetic vagabond), I am sure I would have had my own version of Midnight Express to report. Instead the Italian police were swayed by the support for me of the passengers and took mercy on me and left me on the bus. I bought a ticket from then on after I realized that trying to ride the bus for free in Italy was not a good way to save money.

I have another story of one way I tried to save money that I also would not recommend to others. When I was in college and had very little disposable income I found a pair of Joan and David shoes on sale. They were so cheap and pretty that I decided to buy them even if they were a full size too small. My plan was to break them in and stretch them out. I put them on and ran around my tiny dorm room screaming in agony.

Then I did the unthinkable. I actually took a shower with them on. Guess what, that did work in the sense that they were stretched out. But they sloshed for weeks when I wore them. Lesson: buying clothes that clearly do not fit just to save a penny is not a wise way to shop.

I have other stupid stories that would make you wonder if there is any banana under my peel. Just a few days ago I was gloating that I saved $1800 by getting a second opinion for car repairs. I was so happy that I saved such a nice amount, only to spoil the mood by doing something extraordinarily stupid and foolish days after the work was done.

It all started when I wanted to give my husband a message during his paddle tennis game. It had been raining for days. I should have remembered when I set off that the road to our club is prone to flooding. Why it was only a few months ago that I admonished my husband for driving his car through such a deep puddle.

I had my little boy and my 12-year-old Stepson in the car. When we made the approach to the club we noticed that the cones to block the road were pushed aside as to invite us to drive through the big puddle. A biker waved me on, even though I could see with my own eyes that the road was under water. I ventured on.

Halfway through the "puddle" my car died. My stepson said he had the sensation we were floating. I did make it to the other side (I think we drifted) only to have my car completely die. We walked to the paddle courts only to demonstrate more bad judgment on my behalf by interrupting my husband's game. He was by far more unnerved by my disrupting his concentration than by the sight of the boys and me submerged in water in the entrance to the club.

My husband who is a calm and patient man had total faith that when the car dried out it would start again. It did. Was it worth the laughs my son, my stepson and I had as we floated in my Volvo across what really should have been referred to as a pond? I will let you know when I get my next bill from Volvo. *Update!* I got the bill; it was not worth the laughs.

I am embarrassed to report that I have lots of stories of how by not using good judgment and by being impatient, I have unwittingly squandered money. When I first married my husband I was redecorating (throwing out his crap that I did not like) when I came across an old battered candlestick. It went directly into a box destined for Goodwill.

A few days later my husband asked what happened to his beloved 19th century silver Sheffield antique. I was on the phone to Goodwill within seconds trying to track it down only to no avail. I then jumped in the car and spent hours combing the shelves to see if I could find it myself. Someone else obviously was smarter than I and grabbed it. I paid over (or should I say overpaid) $400.00 replacing it in a fancy boutique in Nantucket.

I never would have grossly overpaid for an item under normal circumstances, but I had to do some damage control. Plus we were newlyweds and I was still on my best behavior. After seven years of marriage if I did that today my response would have been more to the tune of "sorry"!

I will never forget when I purchased a Panasonic clock radio and then did not realize that when the power goes out, it automatically sets at 12:00. I threw it out, thinking it was broken. I later realized I made three grave errors that I am happy to say I will never repeat.

Firstly, I could have returned it if I had the receipt and surely someone would have told me that that is what clock radios are supposed to do. Secondly, I could have exercised the warranty if I saved the information or mailed in the warranty card. Thirdly, I could have simply asked my then fiancée Bob who would have explained to me to just reset the thing. He did that a few days later when it was too late, I had already thrown it down the garbage shoot and replaced it with an identical one.

But the worst offense was when I left my space heater on in my New York apartment for one year and a half. How could this have happened? I blame it on the fact that the control panel was high on the wall so I had to stand on a chair to turn it on. Because the on/off switch was out of my line of sight, I forgot it was on. Even so, I had blatant reminders that I foolishly ignored, especially during the summer. For instance, I would break out in a sweat blow-drying my hair and I had to change Blossom the cat's sour milk every few hours.

My electricity bill suddenly increased, but still it never dawned on me to check on why the bathroom was suddenly so hot. I had many conversations in the elevator with other tenants in similar apartments, comparing electric bills. Mine was always higher, but I reasoned that away since I cooked more than any New Yorker. Not once did I think to check the space heater (what space heater?).

My memory was finally jogged when my girlfriend Anneliesa felt my bathroom wall and asked me why it was burning hot. I was suddenly aware that I had accidentally left my heater on for a year and a half! I was actually screaming as I envisioned dollars evaporating in my very own little studio for over 18 months.

I agonized about this for years because it was such an incredible waste of money. I could have done so many fun things with that cash besides overheat my bathroom. It was certainly my showstopper of money wasting stories. I was not a big waster then, but after that little as my girlfriend Gail gently calls such a disaster, "scenario" I resolved to not let money disappear into thin air like that again. I began to mentally keep notes on when I stupidly wasted money or when I showed financial acumen by rescuing potentially wasted money.

So read this as a little adventure how one person (a sinner), was born and raised a saver and, made some ridiculous mistakes (including a multitude of run on sentences), but continued to hone the skill of a wise spender. With my bundles of tips and sound advice you should be able to save a lot of money without too much time and effort. At the very least, with a tiny bit of energy I believe you will be able to at least recoup the cost of this book (and then sell it later at a tag sale)!

2

Introduction: Penny Pinchers Are Born And/Or Made!

You heard it right—penny pinchers are born, and if not born can be made.

I grew up in an affluent community on Long Island. My father was a surgeon and my mother was a nurse who spent many years as a stay at home mom. My parents shared the same values regarding money and how it was spent. Their sensible spending styles enabled them to retire comfortably after raising six children. They proved to be first-rate models of the art and joy of frugality.

It might be interesting to note that even though all my siblings are dramatically different we all have one common thread besides our love of the movie *It's A Mad, Mad, World*. That is, not one of my siblings is a spendthrift. How did this happen, considering we had the means and lived in a community conducive to spending?

Here is the explanation. My parents both grew up during the depression and because of that experience they hated to see anything wasted, especially money. Money was considered a precious commodity that was not easy to come by.

I remember growing up thinking that my parents were incredible sticks in the mud. I mean why couldn't I have designer handbags like the other girls at my high school. None of the children went to camp; instead we spent our summers at the local beaches. My mother even put us to work clamming. Of course now I appreciate the wholesomeness of that lifestyle. In addition, it saddens me that the Long Island Sound is so polluted that I can no longer dig my own clams for free!

We all had to work if we wanted anything that was not a necessity. I had some standard teenage jobs like babysitting but also what could be considered truly outlandish or at the very least unspectacular jobs. I sold vacuum cleaners door to door (very much like Lucy). I worked in a bakery (which I actually enjoyed) and a toy store. My sister and brothers and I even collected aluminum cans in order to buy a big yellow raft for the beach.

I cannot resist telling you about the most shameful and embarrassing thing I did to make money while I was at college. I went to school at Carnegie Mellon University in Pittsburgh and even though I cannot play the pauper role, I really did not have much disposable cash. I discovered that some of the other students starting selling their blood plasma at the local blood bank for $8.00 a pint.

I thought it was a good idea until I mistakenly wrote about it to my father in a letter. Being obviously immature I thought my father would be impressed that I was so resourceful. My phone was ringing off the hook as soon as my Dad found out what I was up to. Boy did I get an earful. He thought that selling anything that comes out of your body (including organs) was immoral. I was naturally remorseful and decided that I needed to find a way to make an income that would be less offensive to my dad. Once I had completed the final stages of my moral development (around 35) I was happy that my father had talked some sense into me.

When I was young and worked hard at "unglamorous" jobs, I was able to learn about the relationship between my hard work and the rewards. Hence, I really got the tired but relevant phrase, "the value of a dollar". I figured out that I did not want to work for nothing. I wanted something to show for my efforts. I learned that money was not an easy commodity to come by and therefore I wanted it to last. I started saving money early and that habit has continued throughout my adult life.

It is odd that not all of my hardworking friends turned out the same, even though in many respects we are birds of the same feather (we come from similar socio-economic backgrounds). Some of my friends are like me, and I will share some of their tips. However, some of my hardworking friends throw their money around and are heading towards a frightening path that is not lined with blankets of financial security.

The weird thing is that they do not have more fun or even that much more stuff than I do. They are spending and wasting their hard earned cash on junk or non-assets, rather than spending it shrewdly on things that really matter. They are not choosing quality over quantity and worse yet, they are spending it first before putting anything aside in savings. It is as though their money evaporates as soon as they get it. Their money is burning a hole in their pocket as well as their financial future.

Why do they do this? A lot of it is that they have an inability to trade-off. They spend money on everything, without focusing on priority. They want it all, and make no effort to put anything aside for a rainy day (better known as retirement) or even to try to cut down on the senseless waste. It could be as simple as they might not realize the peril of their situation. Seriously, I must be a big baby because if I were in that situation it would be hard for me to sleep at night.

And then there are my friends who are so rich they can really spend. But they do not make the mistake of spending it all (that is how they stay rich). It is often this group that I find doing the really outrageous but hilarious (and dare I say adorable) things to save a buck. I shall refer to this behavior lovingly and henceforth as "eccentric." We will have lots of laughs later when we explore some real life people and their intriguing spending habits.

But, the spending of the rich, no matter how charming, is not what this book is about. It is about learning how to have a fun and meaningful life without shopping for recreation. It is about giving up on the self-defeating pursuit of stuff. It is about learning to be a non-waster of money.

You should know up front that I do not really enjoy shopping. I do not mind buying something I love, and there is no way around necessities. However, if I spend, I want to make sure I used it, loved it, wore it a lot, enjoyed eating it, was not overcharged, had fun, that it was not too hot or cold, and it met my expectations.

You will come to know many of my exploits, how I will return a donut for $.30, wait to get my car washed until I get a batch of $1.50 coupons in the mail, ask my dry cleaners to re-do a suit that came back with spots on it. You may even marvel how I cleverly schedule my haircuts in the morning so I can benefit from the delicious free cappuccinos served to early birds.

Maybe this is part of the trick. As I have stated, shopping is not a recreational activity for me like going to the movies, dancing or playing golf badly. Instead I have fun with money by seeing how much I can get from it, (getting more with less). I like to think that my money performs for me, whether through my investments or through the acquisition of things that I am truly satisfied with. I want to feel confident that I got what I intended, when I spent it.

Oh The Irony Of It All!

Somehow I ended up in one of the most expensive communities in the world, Greenwich, Connecticut. I have surrounded myself with some of the richest people here, and unlike them I do not have oodles and oodles of money to throw around. But do you think they like to waste their money? Forget it! One of my richest friends will spend thousand of dollars on a gown and make sure she grabs a few cups of free coffee at the store so she doesn't have to buy it at Starbucks! There will be more stories on the rich to come.

But even in this community where I am surrounded by some really big money, I did not change my spending habits. I did not get sucked into keeping up with the Jones. It would have been futile anyway since in this town the Joneses are really rich. Yet, even though I might stick out in this ultra-expensive community as a penny pincher, many of my loaded friends take my advice.

You might ask why do they need to save money on the little things when they have so much. Here is the secret—it is because then they can have more of the stuff that really matters, counts, or makes then happy. It is fun, no matter how rich you are, to get a little extra included in the price and to see your money go further. Of course, there is also the dirty little secret that no one likes to be taken advantage of, even (or should I say especially), the rich.

Why I Am Not Big On Stuff

One of the reasons why I can resist all the temptation is that I have kept in mind for many years something my brother Paul told me about Gandhi. I do not know if it is true or not but it sounds like the Mahatma. Apparently Gandhi would only allow himself 200 possessions at a time. If he got a new spoon, he gave away a book. I have often joked that I do this but I only allow myself 20,000 things.

But really, this is not a bad way to live. I got used to that style by default when I was living in my tiny New York City studio apartment. Since I had so little space, I was constantly getting rid of things that I was not using. I did this by donating them to two charities; The Salvation Army and The Covenant House.

This created a very good habit in that I had no clutter (and I felt virtuous by helping those in need). That habit has followed me to my new home. Even though I have more space, I am constantly filling up bags to "purge." This includes clothes that are worn out, irrelevant papers, newspapers, magazines and all those dreadful little knick-knacks that gather dust.

I attribute my trait of buying less and not wanting everything to both the effect of Gandhi and sheer practicality. Yes, I had to adjust to living in a teeny space and learned to pare down on my possessions or I would end up being buried in crap like Howard Hughes. I just do not go hog-wild accumulating stuff (toys). So you see for many reasons, silly or not, I am not that materialistic. That makes it easy for me to choose saving over consuming. You might say that I am a "less is more" kind of girl.

Another part of my personality that makes this less is more style work is that I do not have the temperament to do what it takes to maintain things. It is hard enough fixing myself up and I feel put out by changing a light bulb. It is just a hassle and frustrates me. It is interesting that many of my friends who live in these huge McMansions have complete disdain for the effort it takes to maintain their spacious palaces. I just do not want to live like that or spend my life being a slave to my possessions.

Before we move on I would like to take a brief side bar to laugh over the ubiquitous phrase "less is more". Recently I heard an interview on the radio where someone said he believes in "more is never enough" more than "less is more". I disagree with that statement when it refers to the acquisition of things, especially if the things are not going to show up as assets on your personal balance sheet. I do however; agree wholeheartedly that when it comes to saving money for a rainy day "more is never enough".

But I beg you do not turn the fine virtue of frugality into the vile vice of greed. You do not want to end up like Silas Marner before his soul was saved. Try to balance the pureness of building a nest egg, (so that you do not become a burden to your family and society) against the evilness of greed.

You do not want to become anything remotely similar to those slobs from those hideous companies Tyco and Enron. No money is worth that kind of disgrace and dishonor. How much fun and comfort will those creeps Dennis Kozwolski and Kenneth J. Lay have in their retirement anyway after they have fallen so far from grace?

3

Introduction To The Greatest Money Concept And Instant Motivator To Be A Saver

I recently became a dislocated worker (the politically correct way of saying I was heartlessly fired after 8 years of service). As many of you may have experienced first hand this can be a very traumatic event. However, I was mentally and financially prepared to weather the economic fallout. I can attribute to this my sound financial planning. I had well over the eight months cushion you need in this economy. In addition, I must give credit to one of my muses, a fictional character that provided me with an "epiphany" over 20 years ago that motivated me to save rather than waste.

For those of you who have not read James Clavell's masterpiece *Nobel House*, you must run out to the library and take it out right away. It is part of a series started by the incomparable *Shogun*. What made me truly love *Nobel House* was its beloved heroine, Casey. Clearly to have this much affection for a fictional character I had to identify with her on some level.

The level was that Casey was determined to save as much money as she could and worked hard to build her nest egg. She referred to her nest egg as her "F YOU MONEY". "F YOU MONEY" is the amount of money you need so that you do not have to put up with anybody's *&%$@ anymore. It is like the universal "win the lottery" fantasy when you can walk into work the next day and say, "I quit". But, in your fantasy you do not say, "I quit" you say "F YOU"!

Accumulating my "F YOU MONEY" was a great motivator for me to develop sensible money habits. These habits were set by my desire for financial security, in tandem with the fine example my parent's set for me in the art and joy of frugality. Nevertheless my levelheaded practices have made me an expert in spending money wisely.

My strategy is saving not so much by earning it, but by not wasting it. Remember that old EF Hutton ad, "It's not what you make, it is what you keep". I wish I said it first because that is my motto (actually one of dozens—I love mottos). That is the strategy I use, because, as it turns out, I am better at "not wasting money" than I am at making it.

This is not about living a lifestyle as a Trappist Monk, even though they probably have more fun than we think! I love nice things, like Italian shoes, shrimp that was never frozen, a good cut of steak and staying at a luxurious hotel. What I know though is if I want those things, and want my "F YOU MONEY" too I have to make trade-offs. This is so "you cannot have your cake and eat it too."

So what I do and focus on is I make darn sure I do not waste money. And that is precisely what I am here to help you with. This book is a guide on how to allocate your money so that you spend on things that matter and skimp/return or negotiate on the stuff that does not have the same value in your life.

Let me tell you my style works. I have paid attention to this way of spending, and tested my strategies for many years—with results that I will share. If you consider that I have always made a comfortable middle to upper-middle-class salary, I have managed to save more money than my colleagues at work (earning the same amount of money). As a result, I am that much closer to reaching my goal—the elusive yet attainable—"F YOU MONEY".

Some More Incredible Money Advice—Pay Yourself First

I did not become financially secure by inheriting gobs of money, winning a huge lawsuit or marrying for money and cashing out. I never won the Publisher Sweepstakes although I am embarrassed to admit I once ordered a magazine because I was supposedly a runner-up. Instead I built a nest egg by taking the precious money I made, and investing it and spending it wisely. By spending it wisely I mean I wasted as little as possible.

Here is my first underlying rule and the best financial advice I ever received, "Pay yourself first". By doing that I was able to build at a steady pace. It is very tortoise versus the hare for those of you who learn by analogy. This is what I would do. I set up automatic savings accounts through my company that would automatically deduct the maximum for my 401K and some additional savings. When it was not in my net pay and instead automatically deposited in to my savings account, it was harder for me to spend. In my mind I created a lock box for the money that I squirreled away that I would raid only under the most dismal circumstances (never).

Once I paid myself I would then pay my bills starting with my mortgage. Some months after I paid myself I would not be able to pay off my credit card balance. Would I then reach into my savings? *Never*! I would pay what I could and the strain of paying an 18% interest charge built up psychological pressure that tortured me until I paid that balance off.

For me, it just worked better if I made it taboo to touch my savings. I just did not want to open the floodgates. If you have more discipline, especially with the poor performance of current investment options and astronomical interest rates, then it is much wiser to pay off those balances. But my experience is that when I focused on paying off credit card balances rather making saving the priority, there was nothing left to save. For me, it always worked best to stash that money away first. Think "out of sight out of mind".

As far as what to do with that money you have saved or invested, that is not what I can help you with. There are hundreds of books and thousands of experts who can dispense advice better than I can. I actually like to listen to the radio talk show *The Dolans*. Suzy Orman also offers good solid advice in a very new-age touchy feely fashion. Again, what I can do is help you save money on everyday living so that you have more money to invest. The goal here is to help you get to your "F YOU MONEY" so that you can really have some fun.

But this book is not going to tell you to just learn to live with less. My strategy is to make the dollars you spend work harder for you. It is also not about taking the misers approach. Forget it! Unless you are truly down and out, focus on the trade-off between what matters to you (what has utility and what does not). Our goal is to spend on what you truly love and squeeze the *&^#@! out of the things which are commodities or irrelevant to you. Once you begin to practice my techniques of not wasting your money you can begin funneling more of it into your precious nest egg.

So lets begin the adventure. You will need time and you will need scissors (yes you should cut coupons of the things you are already buying) and most importantly you will need chutzpah, because saving and negotiating is not for the faint of heart.

More Advice on Advice

This whole topic was inspired when a friend of mine told me he consulted a mutual friend (with horrible spending habits and virtually no financial acumen) about an investment decision. The person he asked would give stupendous fashion advice but, when it comes to money, an Ouija board would be just as useful.

If you want or need financial advice please make sure you go to the best source. This is how you find that person. It is the same concept as if you needed guidance with a child. Logically you would seek advice from someone who has reared well-balanced and successful children. Likewise, if you were having problems in your marriage, it would make sense to go ask someone who has a happy marriage and can therefore serve as a model to you.

So if you find yourself in need of some hands on counsel when it comes to making a decision pertaining to your money, go to someone who manages it well, not someone in trouble. When my Dad was alive I would go to him for financial advice because I could see from the example he set that he was someone I wanted to emulate.

4

What Is The Difference Between Spending And Wasting—Would Someone Please Explain It!

First I need to explain what is the difference between spending money and wasting it. It basically boils down to two factors; *satisfaction* and *utilization*. In terms of satisfaction; did the product or service meet your expectations or not, or simply, did you like it. What I mean by utilization is; could you use it as intended and/or did it last as long as you had hoped.

Satisfaction and utilization are the two criteria that will help you determine whether or not you have spent money or wasted it. To help illustrate my point, here is an example. If you bought a fabulous Chopard watch for $5000 and wore it for 10 years everyday, loved it and then passed it on to your precious son or daughter, you spent that money. If you bought a Timex for $39.99 and within two weeks the strap broke and you threw it away, you wasted almost forty dollars.

Anything you throw out before its anticipated life cycle is complete is a waste. Anything that was consumed and enjoyed was spent. Anything that retains or increases it value over the years is money well spent. I risk overkill by submitting one more example.

I just bought three tickets to *Thoroughly Modern Millie* on Broadway for $215. I got orchestra seats for 35% off by simply providing a code printed in an advertisement in *The New York Times*. My husband, son and I went to the show and we loved it. Those tickets represented money well spent.

While we were there (and I went to the bathroom) my husband gave in to my 6 year old son's demand for a $10.00 Millie collector item glossy book. It took less than a week for it to go missing. No one, except for me even browsed through it. That was money wasted.

I would like to end this section with an adorable kid's story, which I believe illustrates an important point about wasting versus spending. Paul and I are becoming increasingly exasperated that our little Matthew crawls into our bed every night like clockwork. He is a restless sleeper and kicks all night long (usually in my direction).

Finally my husband thought friendly competition mixed with a penalty might solve this problem. He told Matthew about his friend's Scott's twins who were sneaking into their parent's beds until the parents levied a tax on the luxury of doing so. Little Ryan and Morgan had to pay ten cents out of their allowance for every night they spent in Mom's and Dad's bed.

Thinking Matthew would be persuaded by his love of money to give up this annoying habit, Matthew surprised Paul by immediately raiding his piggy bank. For Matthew it was a reasonable charge to pay a dime for the joy of sleeping with his parents. As a matter of fact Matthew gladly handed me $1.20 and paid in advance for the next twelve nights! So you see what is wasting money to some is spending to others depending on your priorities and value system.

The Spender/Waster/Money Styles Grid:

No advice book is complete (nor will you feel like you got your monies worth) without a grid. This spender-waster illustration should help show the four different styles of utilizing one of our most dear resources—money. By the way these are inspired by real-life charming characters and I do mean to portray them for what they are—warts and all! So any resemblance to real people is totally intentional.

```
High   |
           The Good Egg        The Piddler
Income |



           The Miser           The Faucet
Low    |_____
           Spending - Wasting

           Low                 High
```

Real Life Examples:
Big Money; Big Spender: The Good Egg

The Good Egg is a spender beyond. She spends more in one month on her American Express card than I have made in some years. The Good Egg is what Ronald Reagan envisioned with trickle down economics. But there are two major differences between The Good Egg and The Faucet. The Good Egg buys very high quality things that retain their value, such as antiques and real big fabulous jewels (she also has impeccable taste).

Therefore while The Good Egg is buying things, she is buying quality, items that have a lasting value (more commonly known as assets). She chooses quality over quantity (although she can choose a heck of a lot of quality). If The Good Egg had to sell her possessions she can sell them for what she paid for them or in some cases even more.

She also will not waste money on stupid, junky, little things. She hates to throw out spoiled or uneaten food so she keeps her supplies low. It is routine for The Good Egg to save on the silliest little things, like key chains. She puts the keys to her BMW 7 series on a plastic pink keychain she got for free, why waste 50 bucks on a keychain! She once borrowed my husband's shaggy LL Bean fleece (I encouraged her so I could finally ditch it once and for all) and wears it as her uniform. Lately, The Good Egg has taken to wearing a 15-carat diamond ring (it looks like an ice cube) with her $70.00 swatch watch. Isn't that absolutely charming?

More importantly, and distinction number two is that The Good Egg is not choosing spending over building a nest egg, she already has her nest egg and it is quite comfy. Therefore, when she is out on a spending spree she is spending the tip of the iceberg not the whole chunk of it. The lucky girl already has her "F YOU MONEY".

Note about the use of "The Good Egg". I do not wish to imply that this person is superior to the others. The use of The Good Egg is meant to be a play on words for the possession of a good and well-nurtured nest egg. However, in reality, this is a truly wonderful person and referring to her as The Good Egg is not stretching the truth at all.

Big Money; Big Waster: Husband Paul—The Piddler

I should start out by mentioning while using code names to describe the other examples, I feel confident that Paul will not sue me for using his real name (and if he did, what ever he won would be half mine anyway). I should also point out that while it may appear that I am making fun of Paul, he is a better earner than I have ever been. He has out earned me every year, so I do not want to make him look as if he is not good with money. He is, in fact, a good money earner.

However, the poor soul is also a waster—what I refer to as a "piddle-er". Unlike The Good Egg who will actually spend her money on things of value and quality, Paul piddles his money away on senseless disposable junk.

When Paul shops he zeroes in on the cheapest things on the shelf. Paul did not buy good shoes, clothes or furniture (until of course I came along and took these tasks over). He will not pay more for quality and therefore had a bunch of worth-less items (a.k.a. junk) when I met him.

In other words, when Paul is in the midst of a buying decision, price always wins. His style is to buy the least expensive item and then throw it out if it falls apart or if he does not like it. Paul does not understand the wisdom in buying quality over quantity, or why you should not throw good money after bad.

Here is an example of Paul's spending behavior. I have seen him buy a milk-shake, take one sip, and throw it away if it is not good. This behavior would irk me even more because if he just showed his sales receipt at this particular store, he would have gotten the milkshake for free. Or, if he did not like it he could have returned it and asked for another one, like I would do almost as a reflex. So he tossed a few bucks away, twice, because he could have enjoyed a free milkshake instead of wasting a $2.00 one.

Paul does not return anything or dispute anything, even if it is simple to do so. When our stockbroker levied several charges erroneously on our account that totaled over $100, Paul just let these slide, until I (the swat team) took over and recovered the money. Mind you, it took a simple 3-minute phone call to recoup that $100.

I cringe when Paul takes little Matthew food shopping because I know he will come back with a bag of nonsense, impulse items. Of course, Matt loves to shop with him—who wouldn't, Paul is very generous when it comes to others.

My husband would come home with huge boxes of popsicles that I know will not make it through the summer, more fruit than we can ever eat, and milk that is on its last day. I have taken back whole watermelons that were tasteless that he was ready to toss. Recently I even dug out and successfully returned $20.00 worth of spareribs that "were overly ripe" that he threw in the garbage. Needless to say, I did what many forlorn wives do; I had to fire Paul from grocery shop-ping.

Note: I often wonder if The Piddler's seemingly incompetence in grocery shopping was really brilliance in disguise. I have heard of other husbands who have been stripped of their food shopping responsibilities, only to be ecstatic with the extra time for golfing or fishing.

The same thing goes for laundry. What wife can continue to bear the price of having all her whites turn pink and gray at the hands of her husbands? This apparent convenient incompetence will be the topic discussed in my next book on *Why Being A Control Freak Sucks* or better yet, *How I Got Stuck With All The Tedious Tasks Because I Could Not "Let Go".*

It may seem like I am incessantly picking on Paul, but I cannot leave out that in addition to these other imperfections, he never negotiates. A case in point, he bought two houses without haggling over a nickel. Paul pays whatever the sticker says whether it is a car, a house or rugs. That is why God found him me for a wife. Even God could not bear the waste.

You may be wondering is it that Paul is stupid and Lisa smarter? It is very tempting for me to say yes especially since I adore the "I Love Lucy" episode when Ricky, Lucy, Fred and Ethel sing the "Yes the Women are Smarter" song. But the truth is Paul's motto is different then mine. His motto is "Life is too short". He does not want to spend time to chase the waste; he focuses more on earning.

He has a point: if I made oodles of dollars every year, maybe it would be silly of me to waste even 5 minutes calling Starbucks for a refund for my tepid hot chocolate. But as I said earlier, it is a skill set and for me (and I expect millions of others who are not mega millionaires), it is easier to not waste money than to make more. May I repeat the E.F. Hutton motto, "it is not what you make it is what you keep".

Now I would like to submit my motto that is a retort to Paul's favorite motto, "Life is too short". My rebuttal motto is "Life is too short to work your rear-end off because you pissed away your "F-YOU MONEY".

Little Money; Big Spender: The Faucet

My girlfriend, The Faucet is a real spender, and should not be. She is a fabulous person, except for one weakness. She spends and spends and saves very little. She is not working towards her "F YOU MONEY". I worry about her future, because unlike me she mixes spending with wasting and has nothing left over to invest for her retirement. She does not have the bucket of money that The Good Egg does to sustain her spending habits.

The Faucet is a totally class act and is generous to a fault. If she were down to her last nickel she would buy one of her beloved nieces or nephews a birthday gift. Alas, The Faucet needs to learn to economize. For example, rather than buying10 pairs of shoes and matching bags per season, she would be better off buying one great bag and two pairs of shoes and saving the rest for her retirement.

When The Faucet moved from her lovely East Side apartment to another more spacious apartment she felt compelled to replace everything including her pots and pans, dishes, glasses, towels, and utensils. You name it, it had to be new and match.

You may ask what is wrong with this? Should her home not be her castle? The problem is that The Faucet was spending money she did not have. She took out equity loans and lines of credit to finance all of these purchases. That just adds salt (interest payments) to the wounds of reckless spending.

After she finished redecorating her sensational New York apartment she decided that she did not like her brand new bedroom. If it were me, I would just learn to live with it. I mean how much can you hate something you picked out less than three years ago. Anyway, The Faucet is going to give her entire bedroom set to her sister and re-do the whole thing.

Of course her sister loves her dearly like all her friends who are the recipient of The Faucet's spending sprees. But The Faucet, who has no qualms about spending her last nickel, needs to know that out of control spending, without a safety net is a dangerous game to play. At her stage in life she should not be recklessly spending on luxuries and frivolities at the expense of her much needed nest egg.

Little Money; Little Waster: The Miser

The Miser is, I hate to say it but here goes, a miser. The Miser is an example of too much of a good thing or "not wasting money run amok"! The Miser is the flip side of The Faucet. Like The Faucet, The Miser has a heart of gold. She takes in stray animals and cries at Hallmark commercials, she is so sweet. But, sadly, The Miser has taken the not wasting money decree to the dark side where she does waste money because she barely spends it at all.

In other words, The Miser does not have too much fun. She not only does not waste a nickel she does not spend a nickel. She buys nothing and is so non materialistic that she only buys the bare necessities such as food and shelter (her clothes are usually from thrift shops).

This extraordinary skimping has rubbed off on her children. It was unbelievable to me that when her kids were young they would be happy to sit around all day and wait to open presents that were given to them. There was just no anxiety to get a gift. It was like the Whos from Whoville. This is so unlike my Matthew who starts an all out relentless campaign to open his loot as soon as his little eyes spot it.

While The Miser's style of turning off the faucet altogether does not thrill me, I think her style is better than The Faucet's. She is not running up debt and she is not buying things without much value. She is not spending money she does not have. She does not have BIG MONEY so she is better off then The Faucet who spends with reckless abandon. After all The Miser is not out there going bananas running up debt. She has not wasted money on things that have little resale value anyway and do not show up as assets on her balance sheet. Frankly, it is hard to waste money if you do not spend it in the first place.

But, I am not advocating The Miser's lifestyle, unless you are really bringing in a very low income and have no choice whatsoever. The Miser could afford to live better, spend more, and have some more fun. Her style is unlike mine in that she practices not wasting money by just shutting off all spending.

My style is focused more on buying quality, or items, which have lasting value or appreciate and by making smart choices when you buy. So please understand, astute reader, that I am not preaching being miserly. Instead I give you permission to spend wisely. But I want you to avoid making the mistake of buying senseless junk.

And if you do make a mistake, then for goodness sake I want to try to help recover from it so that you can re-spend that money on something with value. Of course my real goal is to have you redirect as much as you can to your savings account so you too can have a beloved nest egg.

Why I Hate The Word Stingy

I might be frugal but I would hate to ever be stingy. Does that seem like splitting hairs? Maybe so, but there is a difference however subtle that needs some, as Ricky Ricardo would say, "splaining". I will tell a quick little story to illustrate why being stingy is not nearly as virtuous as being frugal. Actually stingy does not even come close to being a virtue, it nestles up to a ghastly trait—greed.

When I was in my twenties I went on a tour of Scandinavia with my girlfriend Patty. This was not an expensive tour, but we were lucky that it was as enjoyable and as wonderful as it was. The tour guide was extremely accommodating and deserved a generous tip from each person in the group.

When it came time to tip, Patty and I were both proud to give our guide $50.00 each. While we were thanking him we noticed some commotion with some of the other tourists. One woman had $5.00 in her hand and was experiencing extreme stress at the thought of parting with it. She did not want to tip and was making such a big fuss over it. She hemmed and hawed and carried on as it she was asked to give up a kidney. Some of the other tourists were coaching her that tips were voluntary and she did not have to give anything if she did not want to.

That would not have been the advice I would have given. If you partake in something like a tour, and received excellent service then you should pay at least what is expected of you. It is not that she was debating whether or not the guide was any good. She was having this kind of angst over giving someone else five bucks. That is just plain stingy.

So to me the difference between being frugal and stingy has to do with the size of your heart. You can be cheap, but still be generous to others. Stingy implies a begrudging (Webster 's uses the phrase "meanly scant or small" to describe it.) As much as I like to pinch pennies, I never want to be stingy with others.

Keep this in mind with all your transactions. I wondered what it would be like to be that woman and to feel so resentful about the act of giving. It cannot feel good. She missed out on the joy it feels like when you give a gift to someone from the heart. Certainly the pleasure that old cheapskate would have received from giving that money to our wonderful tour guide was worth more than the five dollars she was gripping on to for dear life.

Oh The Bitterness Of The Spenders!

Do you know out of control spenders or are you one? You have to because I just heard that the average American has over $8,000 worth of credit card debt. If you are one of these people or if you know someone who is, then could you explain to me why this group seems to be the most bitter about money, or the most resentful of the other groups?

I just do not understand this, but my experience with spenders without nest egg (and believe me I know many) is that they seem to feel as though other people have money by magic that has eluded them. It is as if they have no free will with their decision to spend rather than save.

One of the biggest and most reckless spenders I know became mystified when she found out that a mutual friend had saved so much money. She was shocked and awed and wistfully commented to me that "if only I had $200,000 to my name".

It's Yours For The Savings

I want to explain something to all of you spenders out there. You could have that money too. All you have to do is trade-off and save it rather than spend it, or stop buying impulse non-assets rather than investing in assets. You have to choose. Since you cannot have your cake and eat it too, you can either have your quantity of stuff, or you can have a nest egg.

The trick is once you have your nest egg then you can spend in a more happy-go-lucky or Holly Go Lightly way (a la The Good Egg). But, until you do, you need to watch out when you buy that new set of towels, new shoes, new matching purse, and lunch out. Remember, when you choose the stuff, you are stealing money from your nest egg.

I worry about The Faucet and my other friends who are spending away their financial security blanket. I do not worry about The Good Egg, or Paul or even The Miser (who makes far less money than The Faucet but can live on so much less and is not depleting her asset base). I also get frustrated when these spenders without a nest egg grumble about how others have so much more. Most of them could have easily saved a pretty sum if they learned to live like I do.

Betting That Life Will Be Short

When I moved I just replaced my worn out towels. I decorated only because I needed furniture to fill the space. The few pieces that I replaced were sold at my tag sale. This is what the spender chooses not to do. They have the "Life is too short" and "You only live once" motto to justify their out of control spending.

This is a bad gamble because they are unconsciously betting that their life will be short, (they are also not counting on the bills following them to the hereafter if they are reincarnated!) If they are wrong and they live a long time, they will be in serious financial trouble because their miniscule pensions (if they even have one of these vanishing benefits) will not cover their most basic expenses.

Do I sound like a total bore or party pooper? You may ask when can I spend and when can I have some fun? Well, you can always have fun, fun does not always have to cost money. But if you are The Faucet type, ask yourself if you are really having that much fun in light of the fact that you do not have financial security. One pink slip and the party is over, quickly. In addition, there is a light at the end of the tunnel for you shoppers if you've started putting something away. That light is called your nest egg, and once you have it believe me you can start living it up (baby!)

I Hope That Rainy Day Never Comes

I have been fired twice. The companies that fired me preferred to call it downsizing. But that term just makes them feel better, not me. To me, I was fired. I wanted to go back and work and they would not let me. The first time I got fired, I received sixteen weeks of severance pay and collected unemployment. Luckily I found a new job, with almost the exact pay two weeks before my severance pay ran out.

The second time I got fired was in November 2002. I got a severance package for six months, unemployment, and sadly a much bleaker job market to face. It was (and still is) so bad that I was picked by the State of Connecticut to receive special job search assistance and career rehabilitation.

During the first meeting with my compassionate and practical caseworker, Hyacinth, I was asked to fill out a pile of paperwork. I had to sign a form that was already pre-signed by The State of Connecticut that caught me off guard. I was stunned to discover that this form certified that it would be nearly impossible for me to find another position in my former occupation and industry (Sales in Telecommunications).

I raised my hand and asked Hyacinth if I understood correctly that The State of Connecticut thought I was a long shot. I was after all making over $100,000 a year, and had two graduate degrees and two undergraduate degrees. Was it really so bleak out there? Hyacinth answered that the state runs statistical analysis and yes it was true I was certified as having a high likelihood of exhausting my unemployment benefits. In other words, I should expect to be out of work for a long time.

The cover story of *The New York Times Sunday Magazine* section for April 13, 2003 described several former Executives, all making over $100,000 per year, who have been out of work for over a year. Sadly, this situation has put tremendous stress on them and their families. Who could not imagine how hard that would be? One story described a family where the husband was now working at the YMCA and the wife was working at Starbucks just to stay afloat. I am sure they cannot believe that this is happening to them.

The possibility of unforeseen and elongated unemployment could easily happen to me. I am grateful that my husband has a job that can pay our expenses. I am also trying to reinvent myself as an author and dispenser of advice on wise spending and the folly of waste so that I can make a significant financial contribution to my family.

But here is my real point. I am so glad now that I saved as much as I could when I had the chance to save. When I was single and living in New York City I was not mirroring the lifestyle portrayed by the girls from *Sex And The City*. Instead I was making mortgage payments, maxing out on my 401K plans and using my commission checks to buy stock and bonds.

I would go to Saks Fifth Avenue and buy two new suits for work every season and two good pairs of shoes. I was not out drinking Cosmopolitans every night and buying 50 pairs of expensive shoes at Bergdorf's. Instead I went to graduate school for five years so that I could take full advantage of a generous tuition reimbursement program. My employer at the time, Digital Equipment Corporation paid the tuition and even went so far as to pay for my textbooks.

Unlike many single women in Manhattan living in a teensy apartment, I cooked almost every night. My big splurge was to take one big trip every year to some place exotic. Believe me, back then I was not staying at the Four Seasons. I was checking into some of the most unpretentious places (fleabags). But to me even if it was modest, it was fine because it was the only way I could travel. At that stage of my life I could not splurge on anything lavish. That meant I even had to hold back on what I spent on my passion, traveling.

My father always said the purpose of the good times was to save for the bad times. This is never truer then now. So if you are in the position where you can put something aside, please do it. Before you buy anything remember whatever you spend is being diverted from your nest egg, and you may need that nest egg sooner than you think.

Save To Save Or Save To Splurge?

When is it okay to spend the money you have saved? For instance, what if, through excellent non-wasting habits you were able to save $60.00 in one week? This happened to me this week. I was able to use coupons, both manufacturers and the ones that come in the mail to save $35.00. In addition, I returned sandwiches for $20.00 (more on subject see Aux Delices), and redeemed my Starbucks coupons for $5.00 (more or how I got those coupons later).

Now the question is should I reallocate this money and save it or put it towards a splurge? The answer depends on the strength of your nest egg. If you have been nurturing your nest egg so it is healthy and growing (like The Good Egg) then you have the option to put that money towards a quality purchase or even something frivolous. Or if you are like The Miser and are so disciplined that you deserve some perks in life you can look at it like "free money" and splurge. Yes, you can spend it—Hooray!

However if you are like The Faucet, and having been buying yourself little treats all along and denying yourself very little, this is a great way to start saving. Unfortunately I fear that if The Faucet were to recover $60.00 in one week she would just run out and fritter it away. Sadly, she would dribble away what she saved.

The bitter truth is she is not on sound enough financial ground to have that much undisciplined "fun". She needs to pay her self first, spend money wisely, and try to recover any wasted money. Through a disciplined approach The Faucet will eventually be able to build a nest-egg and then be able to resume her fun-loving high rolling lifestyle.

I need to now issue a warning about the ever-popular notion about saving by spending. Who has not fallen into the dangerous trap of the shopping-to-save-money philosophy? I do not know one woman who does not have a good laugh with their friends on how she made $100.00 by buying a pair of shoes for $200.00 on sale for half price. Of course, if you add in your tax-bracket the savings is even more dramatic and impressive.

I used to brag that when I looked at all the money I saved in one day by shopping at an outlet mall, I actually made more money than when I worked. But guess what, when I said that I was only kidding. Now, we all know no one really believes this logic. Tell me you do not believe this, right?

The only way that this might work is if you actually took that $100.00 you saved on the shoes and put it in the bank. I do not know anyone who ever took it that far. So why don't we all confess now that it is just a big inside joke among girlfriends. I am sure that the *Sex And The City* girls demonstrated this very logic. But it is more The Faucet than The Miser or The Good Egg and we know The Faucet is heading for trouble.

The Spender/Waster Quiz

Are you unsure as to whether or not you are a spender or a waster of money? Take this quick pop quiz and find out for sure. Circle either yes or no at the end of the question.

1. Do you feel the urge (and then act on it) to spend money as soon as you get it?   Yes No

2. Do you pay bills late even if you have the money to pay them immediately so that you incur late fees?   Yes No

3. Do your children come home with "a little something" every time you shop?   Yes No

4. Are you consistently throwing out food that you bought in bulk and cannot use up?   Yes No

5. Do you have to buy a new wardrobe every year because last year's stuff did not hold up?   Yes No

6. Are you impulsively making long distance phone calls during peak times when off peak is only minutes away?   Yes No

7. Are you buying bottled water at a movie theatre for four times what it costs in a supermarket?   Yes No

8. Do you have piles of unused clothes with the tags on that you know you will not wear, but will never return?   Yes No

9. Is it anathema (I love that word, even though I still cannot pronounce it) for you to send anything back in a restaurant even if you are totally disappointed with it and know you will never eat it?   Yes No

10. Do you keep things you ordered from a catalog that you are not satisfied with because it is too much of a hassle to return them?   Yes No

Obviously, *no* is the correct answer and the more you have the better your spending habits. But do not fret if you have answered *yes* too many times. You may be a waster now but after you finish my helpful hints you will see the folly of your ways and be on the way to building your prized nest egg.

Lisa's EZ Quiz To Determine If You Are A Waster Or A Spender

This section should be entitled "Just Look What Is In Your Garbage Can". Is it filled with leftover food (stop cooking such large quantities), items you were dissatisfied with (hum—possibly a return or money rescue opportunity) or items that you could salvage for someone else (possible tag sale or Salvation Army item)? Or is your waste receptacle filled with used tissues, bones that your dog has already chewed and empty containers that you have used up? If it is the later, good work, you are appropriately producing trash that is certifiably "trash". If not, you are tossing away money rescuing opportunities.

World's Fastest Quiz to Determine if You Have A Nest Egg

Are you able to walk into your bosses' office say "F YOU I quit this lousy job", walk out, and still maintain your current lifestyle? Yes or No? If you answered *yes* congratulations you have your "F YOU MONEY" and can relax. If you answered *no* you need to get back in and work your fanny off, and not waste a penny.

5

Your Money And Your Friends And Family

Neither Lender Nor Borrower Be!

This saying covers about everything. If you are already in the situation where you have to borrow something and cannot buy it yourself ask yourself this question. Do you really need the additional headache of ruining a friendship by getting involved in such a, as my girlfriend Gail would say, "scenario"? There are many options you can go to before bringing stress on a friend by asking for a loan. For one, you can do without. Or you can find a substitute of something you already have. Then there is the ever popular and much abused home equity loan (which I personally cannot bear the idea of and discourage).

The borrowing-lending situation is bad for both parties. It stinks for the party that cannot be self-sufficient. But it is far worse for the lender who takes on all the risk and has to worry about the payback outcome. That is why banks charge for the pain in the neck they incur when they make a loan.

Whenever I have made a loan, it turns out that I am much more appreciative that I get it paid back than the person I was helping out. I end up thanking them for paying me back. After a few harrowing experiences I have developed a very tough skin and have avoided making loans for a long time. This is no doubt why Shakespeare's adage "Neither lender or borrower be" has withstood the test of time.

I learned a valuable lesson when I went to buy my first piece of real estate. I told my father that in order to get a mortgage on my condominium in New York that I needed a co-signer. I was too scared to flat out ask him for a loan. His said, "Well, Lisa if you cannot afford it, you cannot afford it". That was the end of that conversation.

I should add now that my dear friends having heard this did co-sign my mortgage, which I have successfully paid off in full. But, I agree with what my father did and the valuable principle he was conveying that you should not spend money you do not have, and definitely do not hit anyone else up for it.

A short time ago, I proved to myself once again that borrowing anything besides a cup of sugar from a neighbor is not worth the heartache it causes. My friend The Good Egg lent me a blue pashmina that I could wear on two occasions. To thank her I met her at Starbucks and treated her to a delicious vente soymilk cappuccino. I was horror-struck when only minutes after she handed it to me I dropped it into a muddy puddle in the parking lot. I picked it up soon enough that all the water shook off. I was none-the-less terribly embarrassed and was thankful that the ever-gracious Good Egg pretended it was more funny than careless.

Oh The Horror Of Check Splitting

I have a rule. I do not want to have lunch with anyone who is a dirty player in this game. When I go out to lunch with my girlfriends we either split the check or take turns picking it up. I could not bear someone who took the opportunity to habitually order more of the most expensive menu items to exploit me. In addition, if I order more, I offer to chip in extra. This is just good manners.

If you want to be really cheap then do not go out, but if you accept or extend an invitation to meet at a restaurant please pay your fair share. And if you are consistently and begrudgingly paying for someone else's gastronomic extravaganza it is time to cut that person loose from the luncheon circuit (maybe you would be better off going to a movie or meeting for a less damaging coffee experience).

In addition, please be wary about the gruesome task of being the collector for group gifts. I try to avoid this at all costs, but my conscience gets to me because it is unfair to always put the burden on other people. I have also tried to not be a player by getting a separate gift.

But the truth is it really is wonderful for the recipient to get one big terrific gift than a lot of little candles and soaps. So, if you are part of a group of friends who does this, play nice and pay immediately and in full. Do not cook the golden goose, because when it is your turn to get that special something, you would probably love the quality over the quantity.

Why Spenders Should Only Marry Spenders And Savers Should Stick To Savers

Now that we have discussed different styles of spending and you have determined what your style is, I am going to dispense some relationship advice on this topic. It is best that you not marry your polar opposite. Money conflict is the number one cause of divorce. If The Faucet were a man and married The Miser, they would give each other a nervous breakdown.

While Paul is more of a waster than I am, I can deal with him because fundamentally we are both savers at heart. The Faucet's style would drive me crazy and actually did. My first husband who I will refer to as "Satan" was a spender without money. He was the male version of The Faucet (but nasty and with fangs)! His careless expenditures used to drive me nuts, and I was always trying to compensate for his reckless spending by saving more.

Satan was the guy who would always pick up the check for everyone, including strangers, not occasionally but every time we went out. He had a much better wardrobe than I did. The coup de grace came when I started noticing that he would hide his new clothes, so that I would not discover his spending. His credit card debt load was well over $12,000. Even though our finances were separate since we were married I was still responsible for the bills he could not pay. To put it mildly, his behavior just freaked me out.

Finally the other shoe dropped and we both lost our jobs. The financial stress was more than I could bear. Luckily, I had saved enough money for a cushion, and we both were able to find jobs before our severance packages ran out. But I realized that I could not continue to live the way he liked to live. I was already committed to my nest egg and Satan was committed to amassing stuff. Plus we did not really like each other. Alas, since we had no children together and never mingled our finances we got divorced after only 6 months of marriage. Lesson: do not think you are going to change the other person's style. By the time you are able to legally get married your spending style is formed. Better to seek out someone with common goals. My husband Paul and I both value the thought of a comfortable retirement more than accumulating stuff. I am pleased to announce that because our styles are more similar than different we have been married for almost eight years.

I do want to emphasize again that yes, Paul wastes more money than I do. But I have fired Paul from many of the tasks that would suffer from his tendency to piddle. Now that these responsibilities are part of my "portfolio," the amount of money being piddled away has been mercifully reduced.

Special Section On Kids

I have a very strong feeling that my husband and I are not alone when I tell you that we spend more on the two children than on anything else, including our mortgage. When we tally it all up and include tuition, child support payments, medical, after school activities, camps, clothes and entertainment it is surprising how the little sweethearts cost more to support than we the parents do.

Yet, this is probably the hardest and most guilt-wrenching area to save money on. Saving money on children is more emotional than when you save on all other expenses. We just do not like to deprive our little sweet peas of anything. But there are some techniques and areas that you can cut back on to prevent wasting money on your little darlings.

If you can avoid it, do not shop with kids. I cannot tell you how much extra stuff I end up with when they tag along. My little guy is always hungry or somehow manages to get a little something for himself in the cart. Do shopping when they are in school, camp or at a play date, or leave them at home with your spouse. However, if you have to hire a sitter and spend money anyway you might as well take them along. In that case "a little something" probably costs less than a sitter. Please continue to read to find out how to fight the urge to cave into buying that little something.

Hand-Me-Down Heaven, Treats And Bribes

Children's clothing is the best category to save money on. I was lucky to get a pile of hand-me-downs in beautiful condition. Matthew had so many clothes that I was then able to pass these gently worn or never worn articles of clothing on to my friends. During the first five years of his life I only had to buy Matthew a few new outfits a year in addition to new sneakers and shoes. If I had to buy a wardrobe to match what was given to him, it would have cost me thousands of dollars.

One thing I learned late was that many times I would be given gifts that were too big, no one likes to buy a child a gift that will be outgrown within a week. If the gift came with a gift receipt I would return it immediately, or I would use it towards one of the never-ending gifts I have to buy.

There was no point saving these clothes for over a year or two. At the end of the season, I could buy the same thing on sale for next year. In other words if you are going to buy next year's clothes, and do not need it now, you might as well wait until the end of the season and get them on sale.

Children's snacks out are a bother and expensive. I always load up my car with snacks that I can pass out. When I take little Matthew to the movies, the play-ground, the aquarium, or any outing that will last more than one hour, I bring a little insulated bag with enough snacks to keep him happy. In addition, I am good at making kiddie food at home, like milkshakes, chicken fingers, popcorn and pizza bagels. Most of those prepackaged meals are overpriced as well as defi-cient in nutrition.

I always pack my kid's lunch; or rather, I assemble it. I cannot tell you how many people find making their child's lunch an arduous task and ask me what I do. I am mystified over that because it really is so simple. Here is what I do. I often make some hard-boiled eggs. I throw in a small piece of fruit that will not turn brown and is easy to eat such as a clementine or banana. I put these along with a kid size yogurt, little juice box, and a bag of crackers. That is it.

Do not buy those overpriced pre-packaged lunches or pay for bland cafeteria food. It has never been easier to make a school lunch then now with the selection of single servings that all grocery store are loaded with—it is actually hard to avoid them all. Really it is so easy for you and so much better for your children. In addition, it will give you that satisfaction of feeling like a June Cleaver mother (or a Ward Cleaver father)!

Try not to reward children with things that cost money and pile up. Better to bribe them with no-cost activities (yes, I have been known to stoop as low as bribery). Bribery items can include watching a new movie on video or DVD, going to the park to play, not doing a chore, staying up a wee bit later or a play date with so-and-so.

Let's just sum this up by saying children just do not know the value of money. Therefore, if you are going to bribe them, give them a penny or a nickel (this works until a certain age—do not try this with an irritable teenager). When I was growing up I used to trade my gullible little brother Jimmy his dimes for my nickels because nickels were bigger. It is a miracle that Jimmy will still give me a Christmas present after I exploited him so shamelessly.

There is no need to give kids big bucks. I heard a story about a family in Greenwich that has a tooth fairy that leaves $20.00 bill per pop. That is just ridiculous. There is nothing as charming as hearing of very rich kids who get a wholesome allowance and appreciate the more gentle things in life. I was once so impressed to learn that one of my wealthiest friends gave their pre-teen daughter $4.00 a week allowance. By the way the daughter is a delight.

My husband has been doing something just plain shocking that actually inspired this chapter on children. I recently found out that he has been paying little Matthew our six-year-old $1.00 to make his bed. I could save a whole dollar just by saying in an affirmative voice. "Matthew make your bed".

It has gotten so out of hand that when my husband comes home at night he is greeted with a "shakedown" from Matthew. Coins and one-dollar bills are sprawled across the table. Matthew cannot even keep track of it all. So, after Paul empties his pockets, I either have Matthew cart the cash to his weighty piggy bank or I collect it for him. Then so Matthew does not get the wrong idea about the seemingly endless supply of hard cash at hand, we go to the bank periodically and stash it away in his savings account.

Expensive Gifts Rarely Pay Off

I was once alarmed when my Stepson was going away with his mother on vacation. He was seven years old. My husband handed him $100 and sent him on his merry way. I was shocked because that was a lot of money for a child that age to handle. He would have been just as happy with a $10.00 bill. In addition, giving a small child that much money takes away their innocence and wholesomeness. Nothing is as cute as when a child gets excited over some small trinket as opposed to acting nonchalantly over an expensive toy.

I think we have all learned this with gifts and parties. I know that when Matthew was a toddler his favorite gifts were not the most expensive. This year for Christmas his favorite gift was a package of plastic coins and paper money, by far the least expensive in Santa's pile.

So why do it then? I am proud to say over the last few years I have continued to cut back on gifts especially since the sheer volume of the bounty often overwhelms my son. I have also perfected the art of hiding some in the attic that can be brought down later in the year for those really boring days. It is much more sane to do this then to let the little munchkin go wild, open them all at once, only to lose parts and tire quickly of his windfall.

What is the best strategy for children and the art of not wasting money: practice saying the word NO! Get a mirror, say NO, then say it again. Role-play with your friends; have them ask you for something out in the supermarket. Then say NO. This is the best money saving and plain old child-rearing advice ever.

Good News! There Is Hope With Children Learning Good Spending Habits

I have hope that even if my book does not become an instant bestseller, and humanity is on its own to figure out how not to waste money, that the future generation may be prepared anyway. My friends Judith and Ralph live in the affluent community, Scarsdale, New York. They have two fashionable, brilliant and stunning teenage daughters who both have the ideal combination of being savvy shoppers with superb wholesome values.

At a recent dinner, while we were planning our spring tag sales, Elinor told me about her class project in her *"Home Economics Class"* which now has some politically correct name like *"Domestic Management"* or *"Family and Consumer Sciences"*. I was delighted to hear that her class had a lesson in smart shopping.

Each student was asked to contact a store where they had procured something that they were not satisfied with. They had to try to take the item back or negotiate in some way to turn a negative into a positive. Elinor chose J. Crew, which was very astute because they are very easy to do business with. She was immediately reimbursed for the merchandise and naturally did well on this project.

Other's wrote letters and were sent coupons. Apparently the coup was with Petit Bateau (makers of very chic Tee shirts). One of the students wrote a letter that her shirt fell apart and was sent two brand new ones to replace it. Not only did these kids see results in most cases, they learned how to effectively stand up for themselves. I hope they carry forth this lesson into their adulthood, so that they can be better savers and have to rely less on our soon to be overburdened Social Security system.

Re-Gift At Your Own Risk

You can re-gift but at your own risk! I admit to having re-gifted in the past and believe me sometimes it was hardly worth it. To do this act (which also was recently given the blessing by Randy Cohen who writes a column in *The New York Times Sunday Magazine* as the Ethicist) it must meet the following criteria: There cannot exist the remotest possibility that the original gift giver and your lucky recipient will ever meet.

My girlfriend developed a system that I love. She has a closet where she stores her re-gifting candidates. My friend is worried that her memory might fail her and she could possibly give the gift back to its original giver. To prevent that kind of potential mortification, she puts little labels on the bottom to identify whom she received the gift from. She also told me that she has a friend who does this with all the wine bottles that he receives as gifts.

You should never do this with wedding gifts if you have been recently married—dead obvious. I have been given candy bowls and other obvious recycled gifts from recently married friends. It is better to return wedding gifts or save them for a tag sale. Believe me, if you are recently married your friends are on the lookout for this. It was just parodied with a bread machine in the very funny movie *Old School*.

If it is a book—the most dangerous item to re-gift, make sure there is not a personal note to you—scour the book before proceeding. Remember you always have the option just to present the present as a re-gift, have a giggle and breath easily.

Here is a bonus story of how I almost mortally humiliated myself by taking a re-gift chance. One of my girlfriends' known for having lavish affairs was throwing a party for her child. While I was wrapping the gift, I decided at the last moment to add a duplicate book that Matthew received. In my haste I never checked to make sure that there was not an inscription by the giver.

While enjoying the delicious buffet I had a nagging feeling that I forgot to check to make sure the book had no personal notes in it. I was fighting with my memory and kept thinking "naw, I never would have not checked" (I do tons of double negatives in my thoughts). But I could not be sure, so I decided to discretely retrieve the book, check and then re-wrap. But first I had to find the enormous pile of presents.

I was searching like a good sleuth all the while thinking I was ridiculous. Of course I would have checked, but finally I found the pile, pulled out my gift and making sure no one was watching carefully unwrapped it. To my horror I found an inscription to Matthew and now was faced with a more wretched problem, how to remove the gift from the premises.

I put on my coat and tucked the entire present in. I could not re-wrap the gift because the paper was bulging where the book was. Then I carried the gift out of the house under my coat safely to my car. I was lucky that this was not a pool party!

My next problem was explaining what happened to the gift. I came up with some cockamamie excuse that I mixed up the gifts yada-yada. I returned to the party, shall we say, a little chagrined. The next day I went to a store and re-bought an entire new gift, had it wrapped, and returned it to the hostess with apologies (but not a confession). Was saving a few dollars worth the risk of that kind of exposure? Surely not! Do I still re-gift, yes I do, but far more carefully and usually with upfront confessions.

Warning, all recycling of gifts should be done away from children. They remember what comes in and out of your household especially presents. The last thing you want is to be exposed during a re-gifting episode. What happens if you want to re-gift something but your child has already seen it? No need to fret. These gifts are best sent directly to the home of the recipient (preferably out-of-state), so you can be assured your little one will not rat you out.

6

Now The How-To Of Spending Wisely

I will now provide to you (at no additional cost) some rules to follow to keep you on track when you are out there spending or trying not to spend. Following these rules will help to ensure your satisfaction with the entire transaction and help you to control your itch to spend, or at the very least spend smarter.

Rule: We Can Control What We Spend Much Easier Than What We Make

My husband is not as good about not wasting money as I am. But he out earned me every year that we have been married by a long shot. In the big picture, even if he did not watch his pennies, he made so much more than I did that his pile of money would be bigger than mine. So, an excellent strategy is to make as much as you can, if you can. And if this book sells, maybe my sequel will be on how to make tons of money, so you will have more to spend. Unfortunately, I will have to hire an outside consultant for that one which will just whittle away at my profits.

But let's face it, for some reason many more of us end up being in a situation where we could control what we spend much easier than what we make. So let's focus on what we have a high chance of achieving. We will have to build our nest egg the good old fashion way (I think E.F. Hutton used that in their ads as well). In other words it is more probable that we will realize our nest egg through saving money steadily than by a counting on some kind of windfall.

Rule: Mind The Time/Savings Tradeoff

My idea of a good time is not driving to every store to take advantage of each sale. Nor do I recommend quitting a well-paying job to take advantage of every opportunity to save money. You need to manage your spending in a way that is efficient and shows common sense.

When I was a full-time working mom it was hard to do everything possible to save money. I made some spending mistakes along the way but I justified it as, I was still making more working than by not working and managing my spending better.

Surely, I did not have the time when I worked to organize my coupons that I do now. But the truth is even now; I am not doing too much differently than before when I had much more on my plate. Even when I worked I could still practice many good spending habits. For instance, I focused on finding the best sources for my goods, and stuck to my list of favorite places to shop. These were the stores that I knew were not over priced, had dependable quality, and had return policies that were fair.

I did not have the time (nor do I recommend it even now that I am a "dislocated") to run around chasing every bargain. Gas is just too expensive for that strategy and of course you risk losing the value of establishing a long-lasting and ultimately useful relationship with a merchant. Instead I have my rules that I stick to that might not save me a dime on every financial transaction, but on balance provide the satisfaction and utilization that I crave.

Underlying Law: Never Spend Money Unless You Have To

I like to think of this as preventive spending. I try not to put myself in situation conducive to spending especially impulsive spending. I do not go to the malls for recreation. I use the "No Call List" that the State of Connecticut has created to cut down on unsolicited telemarketing calls. I do not browse the Internet shopping sites. In addition, I have also started throwing out most of the catalogs I get in the mail.

Here is a useful exercise on how you can perform some preventative spending. Before you make any purchase stop to ask yourself the following questions:

Can I do without it?

Can I postpone it?

Can I substitute something less expensive?

Can I shop around for a better deal?

Can I make it or do it myself?[1]

Once you have asked yourself those questions, and if the answers are no, no, no, no and no, you can proceed ahead with your acquisition. To help guide you when you are out there in the cruel world trying to save and not waste money, here are my top 50 ideas of simple and smart ways to be frugal. My straightforward and friendly suggestions will demonstrate to you how to get more for less, or even better, more for free!

Feeling Frugal? Fifty Fabulous Ideas To Get You Started

1. Go to the library for books—some libraries even let you keep some of the old paperbacks. My town-recycling center and train station also give away free books.

2. Ditto for Video/DVD rentals. Why go to a store and pay for them when you can get almost the same selection for free in a library. In addition, my library gives me a week, which is more time than the two to three nights my neighborhood video stores gives me.

3. I can live without most of what is offered on pay television. I cannot live without Fox News and CNN so I pay for basic service, but I can wait once a year to watch the entire season of *Sex And The City* on videos that I get at the library.

4. Swap Magazines—my neighbor and I make sure we get different subscriptions and then swap when we are finished.

5. Save on Dry cleaning—I wash all my wool and cashmere sweaters in baby shampoo from Stop & Shop. That includes the precious ones I inherited from my dad and the ones from the 1950's from my mom.

    In addition, if you are not satisfied with the end result of a cleaning job ask for a free do-over. My dry cleaner has redone several items this past year that were not up to par with usual cleaning quality at no charge. Naturally, if they ruin something ask for either reimbursement or for the value of the item destroyed in free dry cleaning (easier to bargain for).

---

1.   Connecticut Department of Labor Handbook

6. Make your own lunch/bring your own lunch. Who ever had a really great lunch for under $10.00 anyway? Lunch is overrated. When I lived in New York City I used to go to Duane Reade (discount chain), buy a three pack of water packed tuna, crackers and fruit from the street vendors and keep them in my desk. I cannot tell you how much money I saved.

    But I can tell you a funny little story that happened to me while I was squirreling away my stash at work. Apparently I did not take the time to wrap my crackers properly and started attracting small rodents. One day while I was in the midst of leaving a voicemail to my largest customer a mouse ran across my desk. I started screaming and while I was in my state of sheer terror slammed down the phone.

    The entire message, shrieking and all was passed around a large worldwide media company. They had the good sense to make sure that I was not in the midst of being murdered before they found this hilarious and circulated it. But once my safety was affirmed, my earsplitting hysteria made it throughout my customer's entire corporate voicemail network.

7. Rather than continuously paying for paper napkins and paper towels I use cloth napkins and dishtowels and then plop them in the washing machine. It is not only better for the environment to spare all of that paper waste but it is slightly more elegant.

8. Wash your own car. I do not do this very often because we are either in a draught warning or my hoses are put away for the winter. Nevertheless, this can be a lot of fun, especially if you have small children who will think of it as a day at the water park. When little Matthew was younger we used to let him wash the car naked. He would hold the hose, pee all over the place and have a blast.

9. Avoid paying tolls if you can. When I drive into New York City I try to take the free bridges such as the 59th Street or the Third Avenue. Sadly due to budget constraints these will most likely become toll bridges in the not too distant future.

10. I am such a pathetic gardener that it is really ludicrous that I even suggest this, but if you can, grow your own vegetables and herbs. You will be so much happier than buying them. Home grown tomatoes just taste so much better and you can garnish everything with those fabulous

herbs. The only thing I had any luck with was thyme, and I relished cutting it and adding it to my dishes.

11. Forgo bottled water. When I lived in New York City I was aghast at how many people paid for bottled water when study after study showed New York water to be clean and delicious. Now that I live in Connecticut the water is not so delicious so I bought a Brita pitcher from Bed, Bath and Beyond for $19.99 (less the 20% off from the one of those yummy coupons I receive in the mail almost weekly). When I need portability I fill a small reusable water bottle with ice and go!

12. Don't buy snacks at a movie theatre. Once the wise Randy Cohen (a.k.a. the Ethicist) gave me moral clearance that it was okay to bring your own snacks to a movie I have never looked back. Of course, I never take anything obnoxious like chicken or anything civilized people need to eat with utensils. But I always have my water bottle and chocolates (unwrapped before hand so there will be no loud bone chilling crinkling).

In addition, I have learned through my own wretched experience (only made worse with children) that the popcorn line only adds more stress (those lines are so slow and long). I really do not like eating popcorn out anyway because I get an urgent need to floss. Until flossing becomes publicly acceptable behavior I will stick to eating it at home.

But please, do not flaunt your little snack bag and be discreet when you cart it in. I would hate to see my friendly local theatres start a crack down on BYOG (bring your own goodies).

13. Pack your own snacks when you travel. Those little pesky snacks that children want are three times as expensive at airport shops and hotel mini bars. I always pack chewy bars, fruit snacks and other pre-packaged spill proof snacks for the kids. In addition, I pack snacks for myself for the plane such as chocolate (that I require daily), and food. My homemade snacks are so much tastier than airline food and the fast food available at airports. In addition, I have even persuaded my husband to buy a bottle of scotch at a liquor store when we arrive and to by pass the extravagant little bottles in the mini bar.

14. Make sure you always have change in your car so you can pay the parking meters. Avoiding tickets is a great way to save money and duck aggravation.

15. Movies are one of the cheapest ways to have an outing. If you can go to a discounted matinee all the better. You cannot afford not to go. Here is a little story about my friend The Good Egg and me. We went to New York City together and had a few hours to kill before a party. She went shopping at Bulgari's; I went to see Jerry Seinfield in *The Comedian*. I spent $9.00 (in Connecticut it would have been $5.00 for the matinee). The Good Egg spent tons more. I think I had more fun, especially since I did not have the stress of the oncoming American Express bill.

16. Use the Post Office. It is so much cheaper to pack it yourself, and send it from there then to take it to one of the new fancier but costly shipping services. If you need to pack it do that at the Post Office as well. You will find a great selection of supplies there that are also fairly priced.

17. Never buy anything expensive in white. It was only two years ago that I bought a pair of white Tahari jeans that made me look like an ancient J. Lo wannabe. Those poor inappropriate jeans met with an unfortunate destiny when I dropped a greasy stuffed mushroom on them the first night out. White clothing should be considered disposable.

    I will even go one step further and recommend that you do not buy too many colors. The more colors you add the more clothes you need to match. I stick to a few basic colors, like white, blue and pink in the summer (with the ubiquitous khaki) and black, blue and brown in the winter. A frugal man I know sticks to buying black, gray and white with a little navy thrown in.

    This also goes for furniture and rugs/carpets. My decorator was obviously not dealing with reality when she ordered a rug for my dining room with a white background. It lay there pristinely until Furby the dog experienced her first thunderstorm. Need I say more then now we have a dark, highly patterned rug that would not show a spot if lasagna was tossed on it.

18. Walk if you can. It's free and will help burn calories. When I lived in New York City I saved loads of money by walking to work and almost anywhere else before it got dark outside. I was in great shape and felt

better when I arrived than when I took a bus, subway or cab. The second part of this is if you cannot walk then certainly take mass transportation rather than paying for the cost of driving—gasoline, tolls and parking.

19. COOK, COOK, COOK! It does not need to be lavish, but this is one of the best ways to have better by spending less. If you do not have time, focus in on simplicity. Most food taste better prepared simply, think grilling! For recipes try *Rozanne Gold's Recipes 1-2-3* (only three ingredients per recipe).

   The best part is you will know what you are eating and be able to control the amount of ingredients. Remember, restaurants want the food to taste good, even if it means throwing in a gob of butter. Control what goes in your mouth by controlling the preparation process.

   Even if you are really busy how much longer does it take you to make your own breadcrumbs out of left over bread or cocktail sauce from catsup, vinegar, butter and horseradish (then splurge on the really good shrimp—not frozen). Lemon and garlic should be your best buddies. Really gang this is the area with the biggest savings potential and with the best trade-off in quality. You will definitely have better for less.

20. Taste test products and see what you can get away with buying a less expensive brand. I am in the midst of a coffee taste test between Starbucks that I buy on sale at Stop & Shop and another brand that I found for $2.00 less per package. If I cannot tell the difference I will switch. If I can, I will stick with Starbucks (good coffee is just too important too me) and compromise elsewhere.

   Update! I just completed the taste test and Starbucks won. This is not an area I am going to cut back on. I will go back to buying Starbucks at Stop & Shop and make sure to stock up on it when it is on sale.

   Please try this with lots of different products and see if there are any that you cannot discern the difference between the costlier and the less expensive brands. If you find that you cannot tell the difference, why not switch to a less costly brand?

21. Cut coupons and carry them in your car so you have them when you need them. I find the best ones are not in the newspaper but ones that

come in their own freestanding envelopes in the mail. I have not paid full price for a carwash, oil change or pizza in years.

In addition, redeem these as soon as possible, before you lose the little buggers. I cannot tell you how often they just disappear (just like socks). So now I make sure they are "activated" not only before they expire but also just importantly before they vanish!

22. Try using less of products to see how little you can get away with to get satisfactory results. I was inspired years ago when I saw an interview with an environmentally savvy Dutch couple who talked about how they kept cutting back on shampoo until they reached the least amount that would wash their hair with acceptable results. Why not do this with other supplies such as dishwashing soap, laundry detergent and other cleaning or beauty products?

23. Use those darn store cards I do not care what those recent surveys say. I have more personal anecdotal data to show why you should get them, carry them in your wallet and use them so you do not leave any money on the table—even if it is only a few dollars.

    Recently I went to CVS, and forgot to use my CVS card when I purchased some laundry detergent. When I remembered I went back to the cashier and got $3.00 back. That demonstrated to me visually that that card saves me money. Besides using the store cards are just so easy, most even have little holes so you can stick it in on your key ring so you will not have to dig for it in your pockets or handbag. It takes such little effort so why not use it? The rest of life should be so simple.

24. Never buy a pet—the shelters are full of gorgeous cats and dogs, even some pure breeds, who will be forever grateful to you for rescuing them. Earlier this year, I picked up a wonderful Domestic Short Hair pussycat for $5.00 at the Stamford Animal Control Center. She was already neutered and is an absolute joy. There is no reason to encourage the puppy farms that supply pet shops when your local pound has more pet "beauty pageant contestants" than you can ever hope for.

25. Do not buy garbage bags for goodness sake. Those plastic bags that you get almost anything in are perfect. I bought this great little gizmo that actually hangs my recycled plastic shopping bags under my kitchen sink. The sole purpose of the rack is to allow you to put those free bags to use.

It is remarkable how you can transform those free bags into sturdy garbage bags that handle beautifully on a clever rack.

The rack is available at Bed Bath and Beyond for less than $10.00. I am shocked to see any of those garbage bags (except for the jumbo ones) still for sale at all. I mean why buy those when you get perfectly strong ones with those bunny ears that tie nicely for free.

26. Do not waste your money on lottery tickets. I know a lot more people who are wealthy from savings and good money habits than I do from winning the lotto.

27. Do not pay for deliveries unless you have to. When I lived in New York City I did not once pay even a measly dollar to have anything delivered such as groceries or dry-cleaning. I learned the joy of schlepping everything. Not only did I get my stuff home for free but also I nicely built up my arm muscles.

    In addition, I did not have to wait for the delivery person to show up. I had my things immediately. I made the exception for the occasional tip for takeout when I was too scared to go out and get it myself late at night.

28. I hate to pick on Starbucks, because the product is really pretty good, but do you really need to spend over $3.00 a day for something you can make at home and get at the right temperature for a fraction of what you pay out?

29. Bad habits are expensive. I have saved tens of thousands of dollars by not smoking.

30. Take care of your skin by staying out of the sun. Okay so I look like a cave-dweller, but I am pushing back those $700 Botox injections as long as I can. Also, I also do not want to miss out on my ability to scowl at my husband.

31. Drive carefully. I hate to waste money on any kind of tickets. In addition, drive slower. You can save plenty of money on gasoline by reducing your speed to less than 60 miles per hour on the highway.

32. Never leave a country without collecting your tax refund. We visited Canada last winter and I picked up the tax rebate form that was located at the front desk of our hotel. At the border there was a storefront where

we could have gotten an immediate refund but my husband and child would not tolerate a wait (shame, because it would have been much easier and would have saved some aggravation later).

Anyway, I was still able to get a $90.00 refund five months later. There is no reason to leave money behind when you travel unless you want to consider it as a donation to the host country. Really it took me less than one-hour total to manage the entire refund process, and as much as I love Canada, I think it will survive just fine without my $90.00.

33. Turn that thermostat down. During the winter I wear cozy sweaters and gloriously warm fleece pajamas at night and keep my thermostat between 58-62 degrees. I sleep better and do not get the same dry throat and stuffy nose I used to have when I lived in New York City and was forced to endure one of those insufferable overheated condo buildings.

There is only one problem, and that is, when I go over to my friends I have to wear layers, because I have conditioned myself to enjoy the cooler temperature. I have been known to wear a short sleeve shirt in the dead of winter at my friend's house who would keep her thermostat at a very wasteful 72 degrees temperature.

34. Never pay for classes if you can get your education for free. I was able to get two Masters Degrees paid for almost 100% by taking advantage of the educational reimbursement program offered by a generous company I worked for. I realize that this is a benefit that is quickly diminishing. Yet, even as I got laid off from my last employer there was still a program for remaining employees to get some percentage of their tuition reimbursed. In my opinion you are just leaving money on the table by not using this benefit.

35. Pay attention to special discount days. The place where I get my nails done has $8.00 manicure specials on Mondays through Thursdays. That is when I go. My dry cleaner has a special each week when certain items (shirts, skirts, pants etc.) are cleaned at a discounted price. It is always on Tuesdays and Wednesday. Why not bring things in then and get some money off. In addition many museums have days when they do not charge admission fees (it is often Tuesday). That is a good day to go.

36. Bathe your own pet. I actually saved my girlfriend and bridge partner $60.00 by suggesting she give her little Maltese Joseph a tubby with that all-purpose baby shampoo. Joseph sat on my lap that week at bridge and had such a pleasing smell. Now since she discovered that it was so easy and free, I imagine Joe will be getting many more tubbies and much more praise on his beauty.

37. I am too uncoordinated to re-use wrapping paper, but I do save ribbons. I prefer and recommend those gift bags that have proliferated over the years. I buy them at this incredibly cheap store called "Odd Lot" and most bags are $.49. Naturally I save the ones I get and re-use them.

    I would also like to comment on the etiquette that has spontaneously developed regarding these bags. Most people recognize that these will eventually be recycled and do not write on the attached little tag. I find that most admirable and want to encourage that kind of consideration and thriftiness.

    When I am really in a pinch and just plain run out of all package enhancement products, I cut up a brown paper bag and let little Matthew color it and use that as wrapping paper. Okay so maybe only Grandma will find this charming, but it is after all, original artwork.

    All things being equal, if I have to buy a gift why not buy it in a store where they give you a free box, gift wrap and even a little card? For instance, at Old Navy if I buy a gift it does not come with a box, I make a habit of taking the complimentary box from a store whether I need it or not. I then use it for those gifts from stores that do not provide the free trimmings.

38. Barter your goods and services. I cannot tell you what a fortune I have saved by swapping babysitting with my neighbor Isabel. This may be also considered a "play date". Isabel and I have our kids go back and forth and we save the $12.00 an hour that we would spend on a babysitter if we need to run out or get something done.

39. Do you know anyone who would be willing to watch my adorable dog Furby in return for my dog sitting services? At $19.00 a day for a kennel I would be thrilled to find a vacation retreat for Furby. But so far no one has stepped forward. It may be the comical face with the severe under bite, the seasonal allergies with ceaseless scratching or her pattern bald-

ness problem that rotates around her body. I should also add that she is a serious yipper.

Maybe some or all of those cute little idiosyncrasies could be the reason why no one has offered to care for our little girl (it was much easier to get volunteers for the dearly departed Calvin the black lab). In any event, I know people who save hundreds of dollars every year and spare their cherished pet the agony and shame of incarceration. I recommend it, and envy those who have such a set-up.

40. The invisible man does not live in your house so there is no reason to leave the lights on for him. I know electricity does not cost that much and to leave a light on is only pennies. But, why not save those pennies? After all, if you are not using the light in that empty room, why not turn it off?

    Even if you only save a few dollars a month you can certainly use that money towards something more rewarding or have more available to pay other bills. Last but certainly not least, you can redirect this money to your very important nest egg.

41. The price of gold is higher right now than it has been in a long time. I just went through my jewelry box and "purged" it of all the old gold jewelry that I have not worn in years. Anything that I have not put on in the last decade is probably not going to be worn again. I am having my neighbor the jeweler melt it down and then sell it by the ounce.

    I was startled when one of my girlfriends recently did this and got over $500.00 for the pieces that she no longer wanted. Now, I want to reincarnate my old out-dated pieces into the much more fashionable "cash". *Update!* My neighbor the jeweler just called and my old, unwanted bling-bling was melted down and I got $270.00 for it. I will use that cash to purchase a small pair of white gold hoops that I can wear everyday.

42. Before you throw anything away try throwing it in the washing machine and see if you can resuscitate it. My girlfriend Andrea had a Longchamp bag that was so grungy she felt she had nothing to lose if she threw it in the wash. Believe it or not, it came out good as new. I cannot tell you the incredible things that I have washed, (especially since I hate to clean out pockets). There is not one pair of sneakers or boots that have not

made the rounds in my washer. I also have washed canvas beach bags, nylon suitcases, and even sunglasses (by accident and sadly they did shrink!)

This goes for the dishwasher as well. I prolong the life of my toothbrushes and sponges by letting them enjoy a sanitizing bath on the top shelve. I even put my son's toys in when they become germ magnets.

43. Buy good shoes and then repair them. You should know your shoe repair guy well. Trust me, he can polish and fix almost anything, but it has to have "good bone structure" to begin with to make it worthwhile. So buy quality, your feet will be happier and you will get more street wear for your dollar.

44. I hate to throw out cooked leftover vegetables like green beans, asparagus, and corn that are still fresh and beautiful. Instead of parting with them prematurely I have begun giving them a second act. At my house these veggies will make a reappearance soon after they first were served in a delicious salad or soup. By the way soup is the greatest way to reincarnate almost anything in your refrigerator.

45. Watch the exchange rates before you pick a vacation destination. Last year my family went to Canada and got almost %150 percent for our dollar. Our last trip to Grand Cayman Island had a more sober effect on our wallets when we discovered that the dollar was worth only 80% of the local currency.

46. Do as much communicating as possible over email especially since you pay a flat rate for your email service and many of your phone calls you pay per minute.

47. I just love 800 numbers. Please if you can choose between a free 800 number and making a direct long distance call, go out of your way to get the 800 number. If you do not know it call the directory at 800-555-1212.

48. Several stores that I have shopped at lately are giving discounts if you take a few minutes and participate in a survey. I did this recently for The Gap and Old Navy. Really, it took no more than 3 minutes, it was a toll

free call and I was given a code that I got either 10% off or $5.00 off the next purchase.

I risked getting bombarded with spam when I signed up on Crown Theatres website for free coupons. Yet, so far I have only received wonderful little coupons that give me a free movie pass and popcorn (which I give to Gail because of the whole dental floss issue). It took me less than five minutes to sign up and now I am rewarded monthly with some free little goody.

Even when I was working I could still figure out a way to make the call or send an email to get the savings. This is when multitasking becomes an invaluable skill to master.

49. I just do not get the whole expensive "Wine Craze". If you are going to drink wine, rather than the cheaper and more delicious alternative water, then be careful not to overpay. Arthur Schwartz, the radio talk show host of *Food Talk* in the New York City area, always emphasizes that with wine the big difference in quality is in the under $40.00 a bottle range. Arthur believes after $40.00 the difference is negligible and recommends that you stick with wines at this price range (or lower) but do not go over. Okay, I will concede that if you already have an enormous nest egg you can go ahead and indulge, but can you really tell the difference?

I find great wines for around $10–12 a bottle. For a treat I go to around $20.00. I agree with Arthur, there is no reason to ever pay more than $40.00 and frankly I rarely pay more than $20.00 per bottle. Lately I have found some great Sauvignon Blanc from excellent wineries from California for only $8.00 a bottle. I am going to stick with these throughout the summer.

50. Is there really any reason to buy Tupperware anymore, except that it is an excellent company that makes a top quality product? It pains me to say this, because it truly is a wonderful product made by a most respected company, but you can store stuff for free now. I reuse all those plastic containers that yogurt, sour cream, grated cheese and olives come in. They freeze well and wash just fine in the top shelf of the dishwasher.

The best part is I never worry about them. I used to secretly have reservations about sending anything home with guests in my precious Tupperware. It was too hard to track, too much like lending money. I consider these freebies pennies from heaven and have hoarded stacks of them to store all my leftovers.

A Special Bonus Category

I would like to share just for the sheer silliness some truly bizarre but great cheap tips from some of my friends and family:

My girlfriend's husband actually cuts a Duraflame log into 20 pieces so he can start many more fires for his money.

Her mother has a friend that brings her own teabags when dining out and asks for a cup of hot water. When "Mimi" asked her friend how she was able to buy such expensive wine when she was at her house she replied, "How do you think I can spring for this wine? It's from saving on all those teabags for years!"

My extremely chic girlfriend Donna refuses to throw out sour cream or yogurt no matter what the expiration date (she calls the whole sour and cultured diary product date thing a marketing ploy). She will scrap off the green mold and eat it, because as she says about sour cream past its date, "What is it going to do, get sour(er)?'

My husband and I actually will walk a few steps out of our way to save a stamp. Rather than mail it, I hand in my Saks payment at the customer service desk and my husband drops off his monthly train payment in a box at Grand Central Station when he passes through. Paying your bills online is a great way to save on stamps. Please, as much fun as it can be to do things on the great world-wide web do not be stingy and send e-holiday cards.

If I have a choice I would rather shop on days where I do not have to feed the meters (public holidays and Sundays). Not only can I hang on to my precious quarters, but also I do not have to worry about seeing an unsightly parking ticket on my windshield.

My husband, who loves to BBQ, no longer spends any money on charcoal fluid. He was given an old charcoal chimney (available at hardware stores) and can start a fire easily for free (and without any chemicals).

A friend who I lost touch with who grew up on Park Avenue had two great stories of thriftiness that I will never forget. Her mother used to make her and her sisters comb the beaches in the Hamptons (of all places) for wood and drag it back to their New York City apartment for firewood.

But what we bonded over was our shared abhorrence to buying lunch (unless of course it's a dining experience). She one-upped me with my tuna in a can from

Duane Reade. She used to buy a bag of potatoes and keep them in her desk ready to nuke for lunch. By the way she was one of the most stylish persons I have ever met.

One thing I did for free when I was doing a semester abroad in London that was somewhat unusual (wacky) was I used to go to Harrods for lunch. The only thing was that I actually did not buy lunch. Instead, I use to fill up on free samples in the gargantuan food hall.

Now I would not dream of eating free samples of food available to the general public, pretty much for the same reason I avoid salad bars. That is, I am too worried about germs spread by sneezes or terrorists. But old habits are hard to shake loose, so it is hard for me to resist using "testers" to moisturize my hands when I zip by a cosmetic counter.

Here is my most ludicrous (but possibly most brilliant) idea to save money. The Good Egg and I justify our entire bridge class expense as preventive medicine. After the famous nun study was released that named bridge among chess and crossword puzzles as a great way to fight off Alzheimer's disease, The Good Egg and I chose bridge (known for its incredible snacks—e.g. the "bridge mix").

We thought it would be a great investment that would prevent huge nursing home expenses later. In addition, we are convinced our husbands would not be sending us to the Ritz Carlton of elderly care facilities. Therefore we want to exercise our brains now, so we avoid ending up at the "Motel 6" of nursing homes.

Rule: Some Things Just Aren't Worth Saving On Or Sometimes The Cheapest Things Are The Most Dear

- Haircuts—believe me I tried saving money and ended up looking like "broccoli head".

- Day old bread—remember even if you are saving money by going to a bakery outlet you are getting day old baked goods. Why bother buying it at all, when it is well on its way to being stale.

- Shoes—Last year's Pradas are always better than this year's Nine West's.

- Doctors (Health is wealth! Need I say more?)

- Lawyers, especially divorce. Divorce is just too expensive and too long term to not get the best legal advice possible.

- No reason to fool with the IRS. Just look at what happened to Leona. Pay your taxes.

- Hotels especially if traveling with children. This is the one thing I recommend splurging on if any.

- Tipping—be generous because it is the right thing to do. If the service was disgraceful than I advocate not leaving even a penny—save that so you can lavish and encourage someone who has provided truly exemplary service.

- This may sound counterintuitive but I buy the most expensive sunglasses and umbrellas that I can afford. Why, because I then take such good care of them. I got sick of constantly replacing these items that I either lost or fell apart with the first gust of wind. I was given this advice by someone 15 years ago and then tried it out.

  Now I keep sunglasses for at least 4-5 years and I have had the same umbrella for 4 years. It beats my former strategy of shelling out 15-20 dollars every few months to replace the lost or broken ones. The added benefit is that I enjoy using a much nicer umbrella and wearing much more fashionable sunglasses.

- Insurance—I have heard too many stories of people letting car insurance payments slip or not taking out insurance on rental cars. The tragic ending to that little oversight is that the accidents have occurred when there was no coverage or after it had expired. I would hate to be caught in that predicament so I pay attention to my premium notices.

In addition, make sure you insure your valuables. I have learned this the hard way. I once was too lazy to insure a watch that my then fiancée Bob gave me (whom I did not marry and therefore is not Satan). When he drove me to the airport on my way to Switzerland he asked me if I insured it. I did not and then he suggested that I not take it with me. I admonished him by reminding him that I lived in New York City and wore it all the time. My last words to Bob on the subject were "If I cannot wear a nice watch in Switzerland where can I wear it?"

That was before I knew the logic that if you were a watch thief where would you go? I learned that when my watch got ripped off my arm in Zurich and the Swiss police informed me that apparently the "watch-stealing thing" was a very big problem, indeed.

To save face I had to replace the watch Bob gave me as soon as I returned home. Of course, I shopped around and found the best price, but believe me it really stung. Now I do not travel with any valuables and all of my good jewelry is insured.

Paul was almost going to do another incredible waste of money until I interceded. When we were first married we took a driving trip around Ireland. On our way to Kenmare our little Peugeot had a collision with a rock. If you have never been to Ireland the roads are treacherous and this happens to tourists all the time. The car was barely drivable and we were lucky to have met up with a wonderful man who knew how to find the spare and helped us change it.

When we arrived at our glamorous hotel in a beat-up old clunker I noticed many cars in the parking lot with spare tires on. I also announced to my husband that everyone would think we were very rich, because only the truly rich and eccentric would show up looking so bad (we were in jeans and tee shirt as part of my never travel with anything nice rule).

After we checked in Paul stated that it's too bad we had that little accident because he was going to have to spend the next day getting the car fixed. His statement was even drearier and more alarming when he estimated that the damage was over $1000.00. That is when I explained to Paul what insurance was for. Since we were insured we made sure to use it to its fullest glory! I called the car rental agency and within 12 hours they delivered a new car, this time conveniently without the hubcaps. Obviously they wanted to spare us the humiliation of knocking them off again.

I also want to say something about insurance deductibles since I often see it suggested that you ought to increase these as a way to save money. I have had to put in claims for car accidents and losses to my property and was very glad that I did not have high deductibles. To me, this is a great idea unless it comes time to actually need your insurance coverage. I have, sorry to say, needed it. So remember before you make a cut, it is not free money. The reality is when you increase your deductible you are also increasing risk, and this is not what I preach.

Charity. Charity could be one of your goals in being thrifty. The more you save on the little stuff the more you will have for the things in life that really matter.

Rule: Try Not To Buy Anything That You Do Not Get Points Or Some Kind Of Goody For

Never even dream about using a credit card that gets you zilch for your dollar spent. If this means suffering with redeeming those tortuous airline miles, still take the darn points. You can always give those miles away to a friend or family member or donate them to a charitable organization.

I just love those store cards that let you earn points that contribute to free merchandise, discount coupons or additional discounts. Fashioned after the much more tedious airline frequent flyer programs (which I use but abhor by the sheer burden of having to actually redeem them), I find the ones at my favorite stores, Stop & Shop, CVS, Sam Goody and of course my beloved Saks Fifth Avenue to be a user-friendly delight.

Last year I received all of these goodies from my favorite retailers. I was able to get free film developing, free flowers and free instant money saving coupons from Stop & Shop. I just redeemed a $5.00 Replay coupon from Sam Goody (that was one of many over the past year). CVS rewards me with instant coupons at the cash register and flyers in the mail with $5.00 or $7.00 off coupons to buy anything I want at their stores.

I also have to thank CVS for the box of goodies I recently received as a thank you for my patronage. They sent me a free brush, free lotion, free shampoo and free nail file. My only question is to whom do I send the thank you note?

Furthermore, I love how Stop & Shop and CVS keep track of my savings for me. At the bottom of both store's receipt they tally up all the money I have saved. To get this excellent record keeping I simply had to whip out their card before each purchase. In addition they also keep a running total of all the manufacturer's coupons that I have redeemed. So far this year I have saved $200 dollars at Stop & Shop and almost $50 at CVS. At that run rate it is probable that I will save close to $1000.00 this year by using those stores discount cards and manufacturers coupons.

But, Saks is the best of the best in this category. Since I began using their credit card, I get rewarded with points every time I buy something. At the end of the year I get a certificate and buy something truly fabulous. But, that is not the end of it. I also get heads up on sales, little cards with 20% discounts off of anything in the store, "for no reason" cards for $10.00 and $15.00 off.

I have gotten so spoiled that I hate the idea of buying anything without double or triple points, an additional special discount or a gift card if I hit certain spending levels. This especially applies to cosmetics. I rarely buy any beauty product without getting a free bag of goodies because they run those promotions so often.

Now that I have more time to shop then I used to I plan my shopping around these events. For instance, I was tickled recently because I waited for a promotion at Saks. I needed to buy shoes and a bag. I waited weeks for a promotion either triple points or some kind of gift with purchase.

Then it happened. I received a card that I would get an electronic gift card for certain spending levels. Since I have established a relationship with the sales peoples they will even hold things for me in anticipation of one of those events. Anyway, I got $150.00 worth of electronic gift cards that I used before I left the store.

Before You Spend On Anything Big Get A Second Opinion

In the last month I have proven that a second opinion is worth the effort. I have two examples to share with you. First, was with my Volvo. My dependable service station quoted me $3000 to fix the seemingly never-ending oil leak plaguing my car. As much as I trusted them, I thought this was a large enough expense that it was worth a second opinion.

I took my car to the closest Volvo dealer, because I thought if Volvo quoted the same price at least their service would include a free loaner car. Much to my surprise not only was the dealer significantly less ($1200.00) but also they were able to do the job in one day. This was as they say, a "no-brainer".

In the same month I was also able to recover what could have been a huge loss in an asset. I moved a gorgeous old Knabe piano with Ivory keys from my mother's house. It survived my parent's household with dogs, cats and six kids for almost 35 years. Then it came to my house. Before it even made it to its resting place in my den, the movers dropped it and a huge chunk came flying off. That was disaster number one. Luckily I was able to get reimbursed for repairs from the mover's insurance company.

Then I hired a piano tuner. I should have been tipped off when it took a half a dozen calls to "review" the directions. When he finally made it to my house he spent 10 minutes at the keyboard and announced that the piano was worthless and could not be tuned. I was dismayed until it dawned on me that since I had already invested the time and money to move it, and it had tremendous sentimental value, that I needed a second opinion. The next week another tuner came, replaced some pieces on the soundboard, and now it is working just fine.

Always Make Sure You Agree On A Price Before You Hire Anybody

I just heard two stories from my bridge girls that inspired me to write something about how important it is to make sure you have a "meeting of the minds" before you begin any service arrangements.

My bridge partner told a story how she had someone come to her home years ago to French polish her antiques. She never inquired about how much it would cost because she assumed that it would not be that much. Her furniture looked great afterwards and she was quite happy with the service.

Then she got the bill. She was stunned to discover that this service cost $6000.00. She is a good little negotiator and managed to get the bill reduced, however in hindsight she had wished that she had set the price beforehand. Had she only known it was going to cost that much, she might have shopped around or learned to live with antiques that were not so perfect.

The Good Egg also had a distressing story about someone she thought was a friendly acquaintance who just so happened to be a lawyer. She thought she was getting free advice on a legal matter, only to get a bill for thousands of dollars months later. The bridge group forewarned The Good Egg. Even our instructor (the long-suffering Rob who has to endure these mind-numbing stories before we begin our fruitless attempts to bid) advised her accordingly. But The Good Egg being kind hearted and generous, never could have imagined that this so-called friendly acquaintance would take advantage of her so egregiously. Meanwhile, as any good team would do, we gave The Good Egg some advice and encouragement to call the lawyer and get this invoice rescinded or at least significantly reduced.

I suggested that she call immediately and treat the entire matter as if it was a mistake on behalf of the billing department. That way she can allow the lawyer to save face and withdraw the bill and salvage the relationship. I will make sure to provide an update when a new development breaks concerning this entanglement. *News update!* The Good Egg informed me that the lawyer told her to forget about the entire bill. Yes, even outside of Hollywood there can be a happy ending.

My worst lesson ever was when I was working and was in the whirl of my three year old son's birthday party. I ordered 30 cupcakes from a ritzy cake shop that were theme oriented (little birdies). I never asked the price. I was horrified when I went to pick them up and had to pay $96.00 for them. Meanwhile the kiddies took one bite and threw them away. Since then I have been making and decorating cupcakes with little candies such as gummy worms or Swedish fish, for less than $10.00 for two dozen.

Rule: Dress Like A European

My former Swiss boyfriend gave me some good advice that I swear by. He said to buy the best clothes you can afford and wear them out. My "style" has evolved from buying a lot of trendy items (age also set me in that direction) to buying a few high quality pieces and wearing them all the time.

Let me tell you this is the best way to dress. I literally have a few outfits every season that I wear over and over, until they practically fall off me. Of course, my friends and husband are probably growing tired of me wearing the "uniform" over and over, but I love it!

I would like to illustrate this by comparing my strategy to one of my girl-friends. We both spend the same amount on shoes each season. She buys 15 pairs of so-so quality fashion items. I buy 2-3 pairs of high-end brands. By the end of the season I have enjoyed wearing the comfortable, well-respected brands. Hers have not held up well. Mine can have new soles put on and polished by next year and look as good as new. Hers have fallen apart.

Cheap Clothes Are Expensive

Remember, it is better to wear last year's Pradas rather than to wear this year's Nine West. In the past every time I bought shoes other than top quality brands, they would not make it through the season. I learned my lesson and now go for quality and forgo quantity when it comes to clothes. (By the way, if Prada is off limits then go for the best in class of the price range you can afford. Last summer I purchased a pair of Adidas yoga sneakers that were practically glued to my feet they were so precious). There are a few exceptions to the rule of choosing quality over quantity.

When Quality Doesn't Pay

- Anything the color white. Buy white items at stores with reliable quality, but reasonable prices like things on The Gap sale rack.

- Socks. One of Johnny Carson's jokes that I still can recall after all these years was that it is virtually impossible for your sock-matching ratio to ever exceed 70%. Mine is probably less than that, and who knows where all those orphan socks gather. There is no reason to buy expensive socks, unless you buy identical pairs. That way once you lose one you will have another mate for it.

- Kids clothes for pretty much the same reason as socks. In this category, I will even suggest not even buying anything if you can get your hands on some practically good as new hand-me-downs. I lived in hand-me-down bliss for my sons first few years thanks to his clothing benefactors.

Rule: Do Not Buy Clothes On Sale (Unless They Just Happen To Be On Sale And You Wanted It Anyway)

The best dressed most sensible people I know do this. It is one of the best-kept secrets in the retail business. By the time clothes are on the sale rack, they are picked over and for some reason not the winner of the season. This is where the less is more and quality versus quantity strategy for clothes pays off. It would be far wiser to pay full price for the cashmere sweater that is your perfect color and is in mint condition, than to save 50% on one that is already starting to slightly pill and a brand that is not the same fine quality.

Time will prove this out and so will I with my Cost Per Wearing Formula. Please forgive the simplicity but I am determined to make my point. If you look at cost per wearing you will get your money's worth out of the one you initially paid more for. This should prove once again why quality beats quantity every time.

Here is an example:

Perfect cashmere $300.00 (PC)

Sale cashmere $150.00 (SC)

If you are like me you will wear your PC at least three times a week. And since you will wash it in the delicate cycle with baby shampoo, it will stay soft and you will want to wear it more because you will not be adding the cost of expensive dry cleaning into wearing it. If you wear it 72 times a year (3 times a week multiplied by 4 weeks per month multiplied by six months) for ten years the cost is $.40 per wearing. Plus you feel great in it, because it is your color and style.

The SC will not fare as well. Let say you wear it 20 times per year, basically because you feel sorry for it and because you are trying to justify why you bought it. It does not hold up so well and keeps producing tiny balls. So you keep it for 4 years, only because you cannot yet admit that you made a mistake. Your cost per wearing is $150.00 divided by 80 wearings or $1.87 per wearing.

My advice is to not buy anything you do not love that is expensive to begin with, especially clothes that are intimately hanging on your body. If you do buy a lemon as illustrated with the SC example, your only recourse is to try to return it if too much time has not elapsed and if you saved your receipts.

As a last resort there is always the tax-deduction if you give it to charity or see if this can pass for a tag sale item. One of my friend's mother reincarnates many a moth eaten or burned by iron cashmere sweater (yes, I scorched one with my iron) by making them into luxurious pillows.

My Mother Swears By Thrift Shops!

Have you ever shopped at a thrift shop? Did you get lucky and find a treasure? Well, if not I will tell you the big secret to thrift shop success—maybe this is a good time to take a deep breath because this is the make-it or break-it factor. Here we go—only go to thrift shops in expensive neighborhoods!

Doesn't that just make incredible sense? You are looking for someone's cast-offs! People who are rich have better castoffs! My mother used to go to the best neighborhood thrift shops (the hospital ones in affluent areas are a good bet) and would come home with cashmere sweaters better than the brand new ones at fancy department stores. Many of these items were probably gifts and the receivers did not have the time or stomach to return them (my book was not out then).

Guess who is wearing these treasures now—my mother! Sometimes if I am lucky my mother will toss one my way, and you know what? They last longer than the new ones because cashmere was not massed produced years ago and so the quality is better (unless you can spend a small fortune for a great Scottish one now).

Thrift shops are also great for everyday household items, especially breakable ones. My mother collected more adorable plates, cups (and even Depression glass before it became chic), all for pennies. It is so much more charming to have mixed old porcelain plates than a new set of dishes that all come in the same box.

So why not make an outing and visit a thrift shop. There is nothing to be embarrassed about because of the whole "vintage" thing. All of those kooky stars are doing it and some of them look great. At the very least you look more eccentric (which often implies rich!)

Rule: Do Not Save Clothing For Your Afterlife, Wear It And Enjoy It

I learned this lesson from my beloved Grandmother who saved all of her good things. They were too precious for her to wear so she stored them neatly in her bureau draws. When Grandma died, my mother went through her things and sadly most of her belongings were soiled or ruined from age. Her whites were yellow, and were stained from storage. She had moth holes in many items. Sadly, most of her precious clothing never made it on to her body or anyone else's.

Moreover, I have learned the same mistake when I save things for good only to have to discard them later when they are painfully out of style. After all, there are just so many costume parties you can attend. Besides, wouldn't you feel so much better if you had to get rid of something that you simply wore out than if you had to part with something that you hardly, if ever, used?

It reminds me of that saying "it is better to have loved and lost than to have never loved at all". Wear those clothes and enjoy them, just do not let them go to waste hanging there getting yellow, eaten up by moths and going out of style.

This advice goes for furniture as well. I do not believe in the unlivable living room. Enjoy your house, and clothes and stuff. Believe me they can get in enough trouble just sitting there on their own.

I will now go off on a tangent and speculate on whether these items have a secret life that I do not know about. I mean how do they get destroyed just lying there? The same goes for my cats, why are they always so tired and why do they need to sleep all day? Is it because as soon as I am out of the house all hell breaks loose and they go wild? I just cannot figure this out.

Beware Of The Over Decorated Home

Maybe I am this way because my parents lived in the same house for over 35 years without doing a thing to the bathrooms or kitchen. When we first moved to Brookville, Long Island everything was fairly new and the children were not allowed to breathe near the living room and dining room. My parents should have just put up a roadblock. I am sure if they had the Invisible Fence when I was growing up like they have now for dogs, my siblings and I would all have been wearing collars.

By the time we were adults and my parents were burned out by raising six kids, we were all flopped all over the living room watching television, eating chips and drinking what ever we wanted. I have to tell you, my parent's house was certainly not a candidate for *House Beautiful*, but it was a real home.

I have many friends in Greenwich, Connecticut with homes that are straight out of *Architectural Digest*. They are gorgeous. Not mine. I have three cats and one dog that can sit wherever they want. My little Matthew eats his breakfast in bed each morning (I have a strict dry food only policy). Most of my furniture and crystal have nicks and cracks. Since I try to buy as many antiques as possible it only adds to the charm.

Baby, my home is a long way from the Metropolitan Museum. But you know what, I am so comfortable in it, and now I will tell you the "beauty part". This relaxed home I have created did not cost me a lot to assemble. I have more comfort and homey-ness in my home for less than those who spent a fortune for their grand estates. And I do not fret over it. I just accept the fact that in my home things with chips and cracks are just fine. It is just part of my style, and luckily my style is inexpensive (more for my nest egg)! Here is a new motto that I just spontaneously created: "I would rather feather my nest egg than feather my nest"! Anyway, the best-kept secrets of interior designers is that the cheapest and best way to improve the look of your home is by simply painting it and keeping it clean.

Rule: Only Buy Commodities On Sale

Now that I have preached about not buying clothes on sale (unless they are white or otherwise somewhat disposable), I will tell you what you should focus in on for sales—**commodities**. A roll of scotch tape is the same whether you pay $1.69 for it at your neighborhood card shop or $1.29 at a discount store. A Kleenex and a bar of Dove soap is the same if you get it at an expensive pharmacy or at CVS with a coupon. Therefore, you are getting the exact same thing and not trading off on quality at all. This is where smart shoppers go to work. Getting the same quality or exact same item for less is smart. Getting less quality for less is not as smart.

First of all do a little research in your area and find out what stores sell items for less. I do not recommend spending all day driving around to buy the cheapest item at the cheapest stores. Narrow it down to a few discount stores. Then when they have sales or promotions stock up on extras (non-perishables). Use the store cards for points or additional discounts, and if you have coupons pull those out for maximum savings.

When I lived in New York City, Duane Reade was my beloved and trusted low-priced Mecca. I used to ride the subway home like a mule with bags full of bargains. I just could not understand how anyone would buy toothpaste, soap or detergent anywhere else. Since I first started shopping at Duane Reade it was located primarily in downtown Manhattan. Naturally it has become so popular that it has since sprouted up all over the city.

No wonder, it has everything, is clean and you do not need to make yourself crazy comparison shopping because most items are priced as low as you could find in a 10 block radius. I hear that they even have a store card now for extra savings! I hope Duane Read goes national because everyone should have the opportunity to shop there.

The Last Person In The World To Shop On The Web

It appears that I am missing out on the entire web-shopping phenomenon because I am just too paranoid to release my credit card information over the worldwide web. However, it appears as if the rest of the world is not waiting for me and has caught on to Internet shopping.

According to my friend Uncle Richard (also known as Dollface) over 50% of Americans go to the web to research products before they buy. It is Uncle Richard's preferred shopping venue and he swears that the web is packed with good information and deals. He suggests that you use the web for research before you buy it in the physical world.

Here are some of Dollface's recommendations: www.overstock.com, which buys and sells overstock "last year's models" for huge savings. For example, they have men's Baume & Mercier watches for hundreds of dollars off list price. His new Breitling watch came from overstock for about $750 (retails for $1200). He also got some Bose speakers on overstock.com for $150 that retail for $500.

Of course there is the incomparable and fantastic www.amazon.com site. They are also legendary in their returns. Uncle Richard says that Amazon does it better than anyone and he says you can really save. He bought used books and CDs for a fraction of retail off Amazon. When it comes to books, who cares if they are used? I don't. Dollface has bought expensive technology books that retail for $50-65 for $12-15 off from Amazon.

Uncle Richard recommends that you not use the web for buying custom things that you want to see and feel. He does recommend it for commodities including cars sites such as www.carsdirect.com, which sells cars for thousands of dollars off retail. Then there is that huge giant tag sale, eBay, which is an amazing place to unload your unwanted belongings (junk).

Uncle Richard (is it too late to add that we also call him Godfather Richard because Matthew is his Godson) bought Polo dress shirts online at www. smartbargains.com for $20. That is a heck of a lot cheaper than $65 at Bloomingdale's. He also got my Stepson Trevor's baseball jacket from smartbargains for $65 (they go for $250 at the Nike store).

The Godfather loves this because he does not have to go shopping (most men hate to shop, they simply do not like the process). Richard says that online is heaven for guys and he suggests when it comes to commodities—go to the web!

Rule: Limit "Bulk" Buying To Non-Perishables

It is just too depressing for me to throw out spoiled milk, yogurt that has grown mold or fruit that is rotten. Thank goodness for the humble banana that you can salvage with banana bread (or stick in the freezer for a good after school treat).

This is why I am pretty strict about buying only things that do not have an expiration date in bulk, like paper towels, cleaning supplies, or canned goods. I will make exceptions for things that freeze well, but even those I like to keep to a minimum, because they still are subject to freezer burn or the terror of the occasional power outage.

This philosophy is in sync with my sheer horror over wasting or throwing out anything that is unused. I also believe in using what you have up rather than having a huge collection of things. I am thinking again of perishables, like mustards, jams, and teas that lose their punch. Really do you want to see what looks like your high school biology project in little jars in your refrigerator? I would not only refrain from buying these in mass but once I open them I try hard to use them before they turn on me.

Rule: Never Shop When You Travel, Or I Do Not Want Anything That I Cannot Easily Return If I Am Not Satisfied

I learned this when I went to India when I was 24. I bought a whole bunch of "bargains" that fell apart by the time my plane landed in New York City. How much did I save by buying those souvenirs—ZILCH! Meanwhile, I did this again in Morocco. I bought these very "Armani-like" slippers that killed my feet and I finally had to donate to the Salvation Army. Then I lived in guilt knowing that I just passed the agony on to a poor, unsuspecting person.

And of course there was other stuff I bought abroad only to realize that when I was back in my home environment that these items were out of context. In other words I was very sorry about my sari from India (I could not resist the unfortunate pun).

Then there was the time I went to Hong Kong with my girlfriend Gail and we went nuts over Diane Freis dresses. These were very big in the late 80's and early 90's. Gail and I were so excited when we were able to get them dramatically discounted in Hong Kong.

We packed our treasures carefully only to then have to drag them and worry about them for the rest of the trip. We carried them like mules all over Thailand and watched as they came perilously close to going overboard when we took a three-hour "cruise" through northern Thailand. Really, these treasures turned into one big pain in the ass.

Of course, the dresses have done nothing but hang in our closets for years, just waiting to see the sunlight or even moonlight. I thought about wearing one to Latin night at our club but I could not even bring myself to wear one of them then.

As a matter of fact, I cannot think of anything I bought abroad that was that much cheaper, or worth the effort of lugging back (except for my sweet little Moroccan rug). The only things I allow myself to buy when I travel are consumables, the stuff that I can use in the here and now (like candy).

Here is my most disastrous wasting money, when I think I am saving it, travel story. In my foolish attempt to save money I packed some well-priced liquor bottles in my well-padded suitcase (padded with my own clothes). Do you think these bottles made it back to my home in one piece? No, they broke and then had an intimate relationship in my suitcase. Alas, my clothes all bleed together.

Luckily tie-die was still in style so one of my skirts that got the accidental treatment was actually wearable. I now have a strict rule that I do not lug anymore. Since then I have vowed to pack light coming and going. I come back usually looking a lot more tired but a lot less burdened by customs, duties and disappointments. In addition I do not have to spend anytime during the flight, when I am already too busy being frightened out of my mind, to fill out a complicated customs form. I usually just put down miscellaneous for $50 bucks.

Again, I want to emphasize that travel should be as relaxing and fun as possible. There is no reason to tarnish a lovely trip with items that do not pass muster in your real life. In addition, I make a point of not bringing anything I would cry over if it got stolen or ruined. That goes for clothes as well as jewelry.

I bring my most disposable clothing. Of course the down side is that I always look like an eccentric aging rock star-hippie-grunge artist (and maybe I am even flattering myself here), but I no longer have my heart broken with lost/stolen/or damaged belongings. Do not do share The Faucet's philosophy on traveling; "whatever I forgot to pack, I can buy". It is just too wasteful to do that.

Rule: Use Those Gift Cards And Store Credits Immediately. They Have A Tendency To Disappear

Use it or lose it! I actually hate store credits because like any other little piece of paper, they are easy to lose. Also, too many business are going under these days, it is best to carry out a tangible or consume the consumable.

The same holds true for gift certificates. I have witnessed my poor friend The Good Egg search her bag long and hard for one of those little credit card size gift cards. My husband once lost a little piece of pink paper that was a certificate for a free tennis lesson. Once these are lost there is usually no recourse, so make sure you use them, and use them all up.

I need to emphasize that you should make sure to use the whole thing up. Do not leave a nickel on it, because you probably will not remember to use it again with such a small balance. Once I gave my husband a $200 gift certificate so he could buy a new tennis racket from a great sporting goods store in New York. It was a subway ride for him and he, to my dismay, only spent $188.00.

Of course he never went back and lost that little bitty piece of paper. Certainly he could have bought some tennis balls and not just wasted that $12.00. I always spend the last penny on those little cards before I walk out of the store.

7

The Art Of Money Recovery

I have often toyed with the idea of opening a business called "I Can Return Anything". The whole idea would be based on the premise that most people do not like to return items to a store, but alas are stuck with a lot of things they have no intention of using or are not satisfied with.

What I would do is pick up the "returnees" take them back to the store and then take a 30% commission. Even if my customers have to forfeit almost a third by having me, or my huge staff (better known as minions) do it, at least they will get something for their unwanted merchandise. I may try this some time down the road but for now I would rather teach you to fish rather than give you a fish.

What To Do When Your Purchase Did Not Meet The Satisfaction/Utilization Criteria

What if the unspeakable happens and you fear that you have indeed wasted your money. Do not despair (at least not yet!) You need to begin the adventure of rescuing that money. Yes, you need to re-think the whole taboo about returning, complaining and negotiating. Think of this skill set as money rescuing know-how. Yes this is your opportunity to reclaim that, which is rightfully yours.

Ask yourself this; would you throw 30 cents into the garbage can? I wouldn't. That is why some of my most "whimsical" and "charming" returns have been a quart of milk that was sour, a pint of raspberries and figs that were moldy and most notably a donut that was stale. I would no more take that 30 cents I spent for the donut, $.99 for the milk or $2.00 for the raspberries and figs and throw it in the trash, so then why would I then just throw these unused products away.

A reason might be because it is too time consuming to return the item(s). But, as I have noted, I have limited my shopping to a manageable number of stores, that provide the best value (price/service) so I go to them frequently. I do not spread my shopping thin.

In other words I am not going out of my way to make a return because I go to the same stores over and over (I am what is referred to as a "regular"). Furthermore, I keep all goods in my car so I do not forget to bring them (unless of course its is sweltering hot and then I keep them refrigerated with a reminder near my purse to take them).

Therefore, with all of this already set-up, it takes me less than a minute to get reimbursed for a typical return. One time, I did not even have the spoiled milk with me. I stopped by the customer service desk at Whole Foods and just told them about the milk. Without any fanfare they told me to simply get another quart and apologized for the inconvenience! That is a store worth my repeat business.

Rule: Return, Return, And Return, What You Do Not Use Or Are Not Happy With. And Get Over Those Guilty Feelings

Okay so now is when I will get fanatical about returning and will give you a little sermon for those who feel guilty about it. Keep in mind you are doing a good thing, you are salvaging money. But here is even more justification for those who still feel uncomfortable with the process.

Dr. Edwards Deming was the father of Total Quality Management and taught the Japanese how to become world-class manufacturers. The goal that he pounded into the heads of all corporations that he worked with was zero tolerance for errors. He is one of my heroes. When I went to one of his lectures I got one message loud and clear "You are not doing any business a favor by accepting poor quality merchandise". Just think of how many companies are no longer in existence or are in a fine mess because they provided crappy products or services.

As a matter of fact, corporations spend millions of dollars trying to figure out which products are perceived as quality ones and which ones are not. Market Research firms make loads of money this way and conduct costly focus groups with real-life customers just to get the information you are providing at no cost. So when you return something you are telling them that this item simply did not cut it. You have given them feedback for free! You owe it to society to make that return!

Rule: Do Not, I Say *DO NOT* Throw Out Receipts

To return something easily and with the best results hang on to those receipts. Think of them as your EZPass to returning. I put all my receipts in a drawer as soon as I unpack my goods and have them handy if I need to return the items that did not perform. At the end of the month I reconcile the collected receipts with my charge card statements. Then I staple the statement and receipts together and file them in chronological order.

I cannot tell you how many times I was able to take things back months later that fell apart because I kept those little pieces of paper (darling little receipts). In addition, not only can you return the item(s) with greater ease and less confusion, but you also ensure that you get the full price, and not the sale price if it was discounted after your purchase.

Rule: Be A Nice Person And Include Gift Receipts

Do not force a friend into the viscous cycle of re-gifting by giving a gift without a gift receipt. Not all stores provide this, but many do. So if you can, tuck one in the box. This way if they already have enough of what you have given them or if they simply do not like it or want it, they can get something else.

If you are returning and the giver was savvy enough to request and include a gift receipt, this is as easy as it gets! Do not just let that duplicate or superfluous present sit around, return it and get something you will love and enjoy.

Rule: Not All Stores Are Equal

There are places with flexible and consumer friendly return policies and those that are nearly Mid Evil. I tend to go to the ones that are known for being friendly. Since I live in the Northeast and cannot speak for all retail establishments here are the ones that are on my list of honor and that I feel profound loyalty to. I also want to mention that I do not own any stocks in any of these companies (Baby, I am no Jack Grubman!)

- Saks Fifth Avenue
- The Gap/Baby Gap
- LL Bean (really the prizewinner)
- Stop & Shop

- Duane Reade
- Sam Goody—They won my heart forever when they let me return a CD once just because I did not like the music.
- Bed, Bath and Beyond
- Lexus. I usually hate all car dealers and every car I have ever driven, except for my husband's Lexus. I am cuckoo over the service department and actually feel giddy after every visit or transaction I have with them. If you cannot afford to buy a new one then you ought to at least consider buying a used one. This is the brand to buy. I know I am not alone because Lexus is always getting awards for its service and customer satisfaction.

Honorary Mention: I do not shop at Nordstrom because it is out of my way and the merchandise at Saks is more my style. But it must be said that Nordstrom has really set the stage for incredible customer service including the most accommodating and legendary return policies.

Rule: Build A Relationship With Retailers

I make a point of not only shopping in the same places, but also using the same salespeople (nicest, most knowledgeable) if possible. This way if you need to return something you have a track record of good behavior that motivates them to help you. The few times I lost a receipt and tried to return something it helped that the sales person knew me and remembered the purchase.

Recently I tested two relationships of some of my favorite merchants, Saks Fifth Avenue and Minute Men Dry Cleaners in Cos Cob, Connecticut. I purchased a lovely wool coat last year at Saks. I hardly wore it and had it cleaned because I buried it in mothballs over the summer and it still had that awful smell. Even though Minute Men carefully covered my gold tone buttons, they turned a strange brown color. I took the coat back to the cleaner who said the buttons were inferior and suggested I take it to Saks to see what they could do.

When I took the coat to Saks I was just expecting them to replace the buttons. I was pleasantly shocked when the manager offered to take the coat back and give me my money back. I was stunned by this generous offer however; I wanted to keep my coat. Since Saks did not have matching buttons, I took the coat to back my cleaners. You would not believe the effort my cleaners made in trying to find buttons.

Finally I was able to locate matching buttons in New York City and brought them to Minute Men. Within a couple of days they changed my buttons at no charge. What an example of excellent, bend over backwards customer service demonstrated by both parties.

Rule: Unoriginal But True, "You Get More Bees With Honey Than Vinegar"

If you do not believe me just ask anyone who has had the pleasure of working in customer service with the ability to give out credits. It is common sense, those that can help you will if you are friendly and reasonable. I want to share my own personal horror story of how I did not abide by my own principle only to embarrass myself for bad behavior and end up empty handed.

When Lillian Vernon sent duplicate shipments of the wrong Halloween costume for my little sweet peanut I called them to get the order straightened out. As if there were no problems in the world like hunger or deadly diseases, I had a tizzy. The customer service representative was making arrangements to pick up the packages and send the correct "Bat Boy" costume.

I put my telephone on speakerphone and ran upstairs to get my VISA card so they could issue me a credit. In my haste and admitted craziness I tripped down the last few stairs and sprained my ankle. The Lillian Vernon representative heard all this and my screaming and crying. She was very sympathetic and said she would send me a $25.00 gift certificate.

She sounded sincere but if I were her I would have been saying under my breath that it "served you right you little &%$#(*!)" Well I never got that $25.00 gift certificate, and I never called to complain. Frankly, I was ashamed of myself and didn't feel as though I deserved it for acting so badly. Obviously Lillian Vernon did not want me to have that little get well gift as well because as I said, it never did show up.

I have many more stories of how my friendly and considerate approach produced results. In the year 2002 alone I was able to sweet talk my way into savings with one of the least friendly industries known to man. That is right; I even got a one-year extension on unused airline tickets!

But this is a good strategy even beyond returning items. Over the years my positive fussing over things has landed me some very nice little goodies. When I was in Canada last year I received a free box of candy from this marvelous chocolatier by giving them an article in *The New York Times* that gave them an excellent recommendation.

My girlfriend Gail and I made such a fuss over the delicious food at Caviarteria in New York City that the owner's mother gave us free mother of pearl caviar spoons. I should note that Gail and I ordered the tiniest portion possible. When I bought my first pair of reading glasses at Trapp's Optical in Greenwich I made such a point of praising their service that I was rewarded with a free bottle of optical cleanser.

Naturally, nothing ever beat Saks Fifth Avenue, the Mecca of customer service. Once I was thirsty so Caroline a gracious and classy sales lady showed me the mini-refrigerator where I now can help myself to little water bottles or snacks. Now whenever I am thirsty I hit up that mini bar!

Rule: Return Things Immediately If Not Sooner

Unless you are returning something damaged, do it as soon as you can. The clock is ticking and some stores, even the most reasonable, put limits on their return policies. Sure you can fight it, but why not make it easier for yourself if you know a product did not work out and return it quickly. To prod myself along, I put all packages in my car with the receipt in the bag so I will get to it on my next round of errands. Since I go to a limited number of stores, I manage to get these things back while making my usual stops.

You have more time with defective items. I once returned a pair of sandals to LL Bean a year after I purchased them. I had the receipt and wrote a nice little note saying that I expected more than one summer out of such a good brand. I got my refund.

Rule: Returning Food At A Restaurant Is A Horse Of A Different Color

I think I was always wisely paranoid that if I became too annoying in a restaurant I was just setting myself up for a food-spitting situation. We have all heard stories about disgruntled restaurant workers peeing and spitting in soup. While it is highly unlikely that this is a widespread activity, surely out of thousands of restaurant workers, someone out there is capable of spitting in a nasty customer's food. That is why I only send food back in the most timid and polite way possible. If I am in a situation where everything should be going back for a re-do, (and this does happen), I just pay the bill and leave.

Once I am safely out of spitting distance, I call and speak to the owner and manager. Every time that I have called later rather than staying and risking spit and pee in my food, I was satisfied with the resolution. More on the how to go about getting a refund to come, including a real life example that you can use as a model.

Rule: Do Not Forget To Ask For A Refund For Shipping Fees

If you are sending items that you bought from a catalog or over the Internet it is worth the time to request a refund for the cost of shipping. Include a copy of your postal receipt. Many reputable catalog companies will also include this cost in your refund, but you need to formally request it.

Rule: Use The 800# Or Address Printed On The Back Of The Box For Refunds

My girlfriend Charlotte married well and no longer has to pinch pennies like she used to when she was single and living in New York City. Recently when I was visiting her at her gorgeous home, I commented on the huge jug of Soft Soap she had. She then told me that she had purchased a bottle and something was wrong with it and she called the toll free number. Within weeks she got coupons for two huge bottles. Apparently, when Charlotte is not happy about a product she buys she picks up the phone and tells someone about it. Charlotte and I are "birds of a feather".

Remember, according to Deming this is helpful to the manufacturer, it is a win-win. Charlotte ends up with replaced bottles of Soft Soap, boxes of Count Chocula and a new Swifter, without even leaving her home. Meanwhile, the producer of the goods gets valuable feedback that may head off a bigger potential problem!

I asked Charlotte recently if she had any more successes. She was pleased to report that she called Gatorade after they apparently had a "flavor breakdown" and got $15.00 worth of coupons. Remember the time tradeoff rule. Charlotte made these phone calls while doing other tasks, like cooking or folding laundry. She did not trade-off doing other important things during her busy days as a stay-at-home mom to recover her money.

Rule: Check Those Receipts Before You Sign

I hate to pick on my husband especially about money, because as I have said earlier, he out earned me every single year, but he has a terrible combination of being trusting and not liking confrontation. That is why it was smart for him to marry me so I could watch how those dollars are being spent.

The following is a true story of how my husband almost wasted $6,000 on an unchecked hotel bill. He checked out of the beautiful hotel we stayed at in Mexico and returned with the bill commenting that it really set us back. I had been keeping a running tally of what I thought it would be, and although I knew that this was a posh place it was double of what I expected.

Well, I scoured that bill and found out that we were charged for what must have been an incredible dinner for another party (almost $6,000 for dinner for four). Once I made that discovery I raced up to the checkout desk and hovered around for about 20 minutes. They figured out that the charge was erroneous and re-assigned it to the proper guest. In the meantime, I used that extra time while I was hovering to notice another charge that was billed twice and got another $28.00 credit.

My husband was embarrassed as he should have been for not being more prudent, and I of course was exasperated that I had now secured another official role for the rest of my life "Checker of the Bills" in addition to "Official Food Shopper".

I always check bills and receipts before I leave the store. I rarely find mistakes in most retail stores (if I do it is usually an item that has been marked down or on sale that I did not get the discounted price for). However, I have been known to pick up some slack at restaurants. Last year I saved $12.00 at one restaurant because I was charged for two martinis rather than one (and believe me if I had that second martini I would not have been able to check that bill). I have many more restaurant examples but I am sure you get the point.

Rule: Procrastination Is The Devils (Or Creditors) Nectar

Late charges are an unbelievable waste of money, especially if you are paying for something already on credit. On top of 18% interest fees, do you really need to pay an additional dollar because you forgot to make your payment on time? In order to make sure you do not forget to pay bills remit as soon as they come in. Credit Card companies are reducing the cycle to a few weeks rather than a month; so do not bother worrying about float. If you cannot pay them as soon as they come in, keep shuffling through bills at least 3 times a week to stay on top of them.

If you are incurring late charges because you just cannot pay, then you need to do serious debt reduction planning. First thing, cut the spending faucet and then make sure you are not wasting a thing that you buy. Why not take advantage of the auto-pay services that automatically link to your checking account as a last resort if you cannot pay on time?

I make sure to pay my bills on time. But once in a while, something will slip through. Once every two years I have been late paying my condo unit maintenance fees and I am embarrassed to say that once I was late paying my beloved Saks Fifth Avenue invoice. In all cases, I called and apologized for being late. I also pointed out that I have proven to be a consistently timely remitter. The late fees were waived. But keep in mind both of these businesses were inclined to graciously waive the charges because I had established a good track record of paying on time.

Rule: I Am Ready To Beat The Dead Horse About Those Crazy Interest Rates

Look there is no way I think this is a new idea but really, once you have paid yourself first do you then really want to pay rates that are so out of whack with the rest of what the economy is doing? Credit cards rates are in a time warp and still behave as if this is the 1980s.

Here is a question I found on the Motley Fool website that really brings the point home: "Can you afford to set aside just 10 bucks a week? Over the course of 15 years, you could pile up more than $11,600 in savings (assuming a 6% annual rate of return). By contrast, spending $10 a week on a credit card charging 18% interest will leave you owing $40,000." Ouch! Now stop the ultimate waste of money and stop buying on credit, and use some discipline to get rid of that ludicrous debt (sorry, but someone had to say it).

Rule: Mange Your Receivables

Manage your insurance claims. Did you ever read the book or see the movie *The Rainmaker* written by John Grisham? You should because it is a real eye-opener. The story reveals how some unscrupulous insurance companies deliberately use tactics to delay reimbursements so that frustrated claimants eventually give up.

I have long been suspicious that those whose claims get paid are those who track them. Make sure your claims are submitted as soon as you incur an expense, so that you do not lose the paperwork or lose more of the time it takes for the refund.

This is what I do with all my receivables. I have two folders; one for insurance claims (the largest chunk of receivables) and another for general receivables that I am expecting, refunds on non-medical claims. A recent example is the company that moved my piano dropped it. I submitted a claim for $125.00 that I saw through to completion. If you are really organized you can do what my girlfriend Lita does, and put all of your receivables on an Excel Spreadsheet.

I thought is was just as easy to plunk them in a folder and look through them at least once a month to make sure nothing fell through the cracks. When they are paid I pull that paperwork and put it in a permanent file. If it is a one-time transaction with a company and you are not going to do repeated business with you can just toss the paperwork. Because I am constantly culling, I am only looking through the unpaid papers and the task is less daunting.

Remember insurance companies and other businesses do not expect you to do this! It is like gift certificates, they like to float your money. That's is why it is essential you track the reimbursements that are owed to you.

Don't forget your expense account either. When I used to have an expense account (oh how I miss those glory days), I stayed on top of every little expense. At the end of every workday if I incurred any expense, no matter how trivial I would tape the receipt to a blank piece of paper and put it in a folder. This way I would not lose out on a single penny I was owed. I never missed out on a $.37 stamp or $3.00 toll reimbursement.

Moreover, I made sure that they were submitted in a timely fashion, especially since I was out of the cash and the company had to reimburse me. It used to amaze me how many of my coworkers either did not keep track of what they were spending and therefore lost out on the reimbursement or submitted them so late and let their account receivables grow and grow. I also had this awful premonition that these same people could have used the money they were owed to pay off debt that they were paying interest on. That is just mind-boggling!

Rule: Send In Your Rebates As Soon As You Take The Thing Out Of The Box

Rebates are like found money. They are like coupons but for much higher dollar values. I just got $100.00 back on a Hewlett Packard printer. If you have 2 minutes to spare, or do not but can multitask, please do not forget to send these in. The longer you wait the less likely you will do this and you add on the risk that the offer will expire. You even risk that the company making the offer will go out of business (not a joke in this economy).

In addition, you need to manage these as you do all your receivables, by constantly checking their progress and calling to follow-up after a few months have passed. Keep in mind most rebate offers will give you an idea of how long it will take, so mark that on your paperwork for follow-up. There is no reason to start calling after one month if the offer implies it could take 6-8 weeks.

Rule: Go Over Your Charge Card Statements With A Fine Tooth Comb. They Are A Playland For Scams

Make sure you always go over all your charge card statements. A few months ago there was a charge on my monthly statement for an "Autoexpress800" service for $69.99. I called the number and they wanted to get a whole bunch of information from me and I immediately realized it was a scam. I called VISA as soon as I got off the phone and asked to dispute the charge. Within 60 days it was off my statement and I received full credit for the $69.99.

Make sure that you do not wait too long to file any kind of dispute. Most credit card companies have a time limit on when they will accept disputes. If I was not on my toes and did not scour my statement this scam operation would have had $69.99 of my money. If I had procrastinated and realized this a few months later I would have still lost out on the credit reversal.

Rule: Get On The "*No Call List*"

To avoid stupid telemarketing impulse purchases like when my husband bought $60.00 of light bulbs or I grossly overpaid for frozen steaks, either screen your calls, get caller ID or better yet, get on your state's No Call List. I have made a rule not to accept any telephone solicitations. This rule prevents me from acting impulsively and buying something unexpected over the phone. I try hard to avoid these calls. Plus my home is already noisy enough.

I was able to register for the No Call List on the State of Connecticut Department of Consumer Protection's website. Since I registered almost one year ago there has been breaking news that there is a new website www.donotcall.gov that will do this quickly for you.

As if life is not cruel enough, I add to the hostility by saying to any telemarketing caller "I am on the No Call List, please take me off your list immediately". Alas, my tone is often snotty. If the telemarketer continues to call and if I am really grumpy I tell them that I will report them. They can then get a penalty. Since I got on the list the number of calls I normally would receive has dropped. Heartless, I think a little bit, but if I am not intending to buy anything from them why waste their time.

One of my awful summer jobs was calling for magazine subscriptions. The place was a fly-by-night and I was a naïve teenager, barely working for minimum wage. Still there was no point in allowing this kind of intrusion to continue just because I envisioned a little a mini me on the other side of the phone.

By the way since I have the free No Call List service provided by my state I do not need to spend a few dollars every month to get Caller ID. Before I knew about the No Call List I tried to get Caller ID but I was too much of a Luddite to figure it out and sent the device back. Frankly, who really needs that unless you are running and hiding from your creditors and if you follow my advice it will not be a problem.

Rule: Never Pay To Fix Anything That Would Cost You About The Same To Replace

The latest example that comes to my mind (and still irritates me to no end) is when my husband spent over $350 to replace batteries for our video camera. What was beyond reason was that this purchase was for a camera over 5 years old. It just so happens that new, more advanced ones (digital) by the same manufacturer were available for nearly the same price as the new batteries.

This was a silly expenditure for my husband, but remember he is the better earner, I am the wiser spender. When it comes to technology that becomes outdated at a very rapid pace, once something breaks (unless it is a minor charge to fix), you are better off tossing and replacing.

You may ask, then what do you fix? The easy answer is something that is irreplaceable, an antique or family heirloom, not obsolete or already upgraded, or when fixing it is a small fraction of the cost. I do repair good shoes and handbags, moth holes on good cashmere sweaters, jewelry, furniture that is in good condition or anything antique. Of course I am always fixing my body, my teeth my hair, and my skin. It is, after all, antique and irreplaceable!

Technology is the big money pit and hardly ever worth it. Any products such as televisions, VCRs, cell phones, microwaves are probably lower in price then when you bought them and most likely replaced by more advanced models. Remember only fix it if it is such an insignificant price and convenient. However, that is rarely the case. I cannot personally think of when it made sense in my lifetime to fix anything in this category.

Check Those Warranties

But first see if you can get it replaced through a warranty. Make sure you fill out and send in all warranty information. In most cases, that gives you a free year of protection. If it breaks after the warranty period and was sufficiently used, and you lost your receipt and have no relationship with the store, try to sell it at a tag sale. A fix-it type may want it. If none of these options work then toss it, and sink your money into a newer one. Don't sink more into a loser.

I have had very good luck exercising the warranty on appliances, my cars and even services such as professional scotch guarding. Here is a real life example of how I exercised a warranty I had for a service.

When I decorated my home, I had all my furniture with fabric treated with scotch guard. It all worked well under the real-life unrehearsed testing of children, pets and clumsy parents. However, Matthew managed to spill milk from his ba-ba and it stained one of the chairs. After I unsuccessfully tried to remove the stains myself, I called the service that did the scotch guarding. They sent someone who tried to remove the stain. It did not work, so they refunded the entire amount of the fee we paid. It was $175.00.

A Special End Of The Chapter Treat For My Delightful Readers And The Piece De Resistance: My Most Outrageous Return Story—Billy Martins

This is my most accomplished and outrageous return story. It happened more than a decade ago. There used to be a swanky store on Madison Avenue called Billy Martins. In the height of the Western Boot craze I heard that you could get Justin boots (a terrific long-lasting brand) through an 800 number (1800-4Justin) at a significant discount. But in order to do this and be sure you were getting the pair you had in mind, it was best to have the style number.

So I went in to Billy Martins known for its selection of Western attire, tried on boots and began to write down the style number. Of course, the sales clerk was on to this little scheme, and offered to discount the boots on the spot. Certainly I took her offer and went home with the discounted boots.

Sadly, I did not do my due diligence and learned after I walked to my graduate school and back home, that when you buy cowboy boots you are supposed to go down a full size. My bargain boots were flopping around my feet. So, I promptly took them back to Billy Martins receipt in hand.

I was much younger then, or maybe I would have had more shame, because clearly this was a caveat emptor situation. The boots were not defective. Still, undeterred I ventured on and tried to return the boots on the grounds that I was in fact a knucklehead and the salesperson was the expert and should have advised me about the sizing discrepancy.

Well, they did not buy my argument. So, hating to be out that kind of money with un-wearable boots I proceeded, in full view the manager and employees to try to sell my boots to the other customers. This was chutzpah out of control and if it was not so ludicrous I would be embarrassed. However, within 15 minutes I had sold my gently worn boots to a friend of a friend right in the store.

But the best part is that later that day I received a call from a representative of the store. Rather than being outraged, they were amused and invited me back in to buy another pair at a discount. I went back in, got my boots, made nice-nice with everyone and had a great silly story to tell.

More good free press a propos to Billy Martins. I also have heard on Don Imus that this fabulous fun-loving store also donates hundreds of these durable Justin boots every year to his charity—the Don Imus Ranch for children with cancer. Goodwill and kindness run deep (not to mention a world class sense of humor).

8

Get Ready! At Some Point In Time You Will Need To Negotiate!

I took this amazing Negotiations Class in the spring of 2002 by a company called Scotworks. It was the first time ever that I did not spend my time in one of those tedious corporate training classes cleaning out my purse or working on my To Do list. But if I could sum up an exquisite three day learning extravaganza down to one sentence it would be this: "If you do this for me, then I will do this for you". We condensed this to the more efficient sound bite of the "Big If—Then". It sounds a lot like I will scratch your back if you scratch mine, and it works.

There are many great books on Negotiation such as Herb Cohen's, *You Can Negotiate Anything.* Of course anyone who can take the Scotworks class must (you can find out more by contacting them at **usa@scotwork.com**). But my take on this topic and what I am going to submit to you is that when you are trying to negotiate or get something resolved with a business, keep in mind when you are asking "If you do this for me" you are implying the then for them.

If the "if" for you is your money back, another item from the store, a do-over or a credit then the "then" for them is that you will continue to do business with them. Moreover you will be a loyal and enthusiastic customer who will be happy to give them free and fantastic publicity. In addition, the "then" is that you will also make them look good in front of other shoppers.

Although I have not had to do the literal "Big If—Then" too often, I let the spirit of the implied trade-off inspire me to act. This may sound a little mercenary but this is all very Pavlovian. If the merchant is good, they get your return business. On the other hand if the merchant is bad, you walk out forever and they miss the happy stream of potential business. I will share a list that may surprise you of how easy the implied "Big If-Then" can be.

Here is a list of items I was able to negotiate over the last year and the subsequent savings or wasted money I recovered. Remember nothing ventured nothing gained.

- When I was laid off I lost my company's employee paid wireless services. Alas, I had to open two new accounts, one for my husband and one for me. Somehow I misunderstood that my husband's plan did not include local roaming. When the first bill came in and I realized that he was on the wrong plan, I immediately called AT&T Wireless Services and asked if they would retroactively put my husband's account on the most suitable plan for his calling pattern. I made some kind of self-deprecating joke about a stupid persons discount. I was careful to make sure my approach was to blame myself and ask for mercy. It worked because I was given a $38.00 credit and placed on the optimal plan. This took about 10 minutes.

- Midwest Airlines was kind enough to extend unused tickets for an additional year, representing a savings of almost $690.00. Most airline policies provide a one-year extension for unused tickets. This meant spending some time explaining why we could not use them within one year. We did have a very good reason, so if you do too, it is worth a try.

- I received a bill from my oil company that I thought was over the top for repair work done on my furnace. I called the company and politely asked for an explanation. After the representative respectfully explained the details of the bill, I commented that even though I understood the bill better I still found it expensive. She then said that she would reduce the bill by $100.00. Of course I thanked her profusely for her kindness.

- My husband and I went to dinner at this lovely restaurant, The Willet House. We were surprised though that that particular meal was not up to the standards we expected. In this case, since we still had such a delightful night we paid the bill and tipped and left. When the Visa bill arrived and I saw the $170.00 charge I just did not feel good about it, so I took the chance and called the manager of the restaurant. I knew that it was a long shot, because the bill was paid weeks ago. Since I did not have much wiggle room, I had no choice but to position my call as being helpful.

  I told the manager that although the service and atmosphere was just fine, it was not comparable to other steak houses in its category. Without even raising my voice one decibel the owner asked that we come back in and let them make it up to us. They sent a letter confirming their offer. My husband and I went back for a free delicious meal and now have a very positive attitude towards that classy establishment.

Lesson, first handle the situation then and there, but if you do not, it is worth the effort to call and discuss it with them in a helpful manner. Any business that is worthwhile continuing a relationship with will try to remedy the situation to your satisfaction.

- I had a bad haircut redone at no cost. My hairdresser Giancarlo is usually magnificent and well respected in my community. When he gave me a haircut that just did not "wash", I called him back (it was even a few weeks after the cut). Rather than risk my continued business he was happy to cut my hair again at no cost. By the way, his salon makes the most delicious cappuccino, which I make sure to get whenever I am there. This is when I will reveal my tendency to only schedule early morning appointments so I can take full advantage of the scrumptious hot beverage.

- When Cablevision was hours late to install my Internet connection I called customer service to find out whether or not they were still coming. I expressed my frustration with waiting around all day for them. I also let them know that this did not create a good impression on their part. The representative on the phone immediately offered a free month service. This was a savings of $39.00.

- It was entirely my fault when I took in a cushion to be repaired at S&S Cleaners and did not carefully read the work order. I thought the minor repair would only be $2.50. When I went to pick up my cleaning order and after the cashier totaled my bill it turned out that the repair work was $25.00. When I found this out I asked to speak to the manager.

This is how I proceeded. Rather than be angry (it was my fault for not taking the time to read carefully), I asked if he could just look at what I paid $25.00 for. I "fessed-up" by saying that this in no way was S&S's fault because I clearly see now that the charge was on the bill.

However, I asked the manager if we could meet half way because it was just so much for such a little job. He then explained to me that it was the minimum charge for all repair work, however, since it was such a small job he offered to waive the $25.00 charge. I am sure it did not hurt my cause that I was reasonable in my request.

- I adore Cinnabons. But once I got a box that I did not think was as fresh and delicious as they usually are. I called toll-free information (800) 555-1212 and got Cinnabon's toll free number. I called the customer service department and explained the situation. Within a few weeks I received a coupon for a free box of Cinnabons.

- Starbucks is another company that is truly committed to customer satisfaction. I am crazy about hot chocolate so when I was beginning to consistently get hot chocolates that were room temperature, I called the Starbucks toll-free number and explained the situation in the nicest voice I could muster. I was also curious as to whether or not it was deliberate after the big McDonalds hot coffee spilled on lap lawsuit (it was not).

  I was pleasantly surprised when I was told the coupons for two free drinks were on the way (well not really that surprised because I have learned that this friendly helpful approach is often rewarded). Within a few days I received two coupons for free beverages and the sweetest letter thanking me for my valuable feedback.

- I took my son to Stamford Raceway to race slot cars last year. I did not realize at the time that different courses had different charges. Anyway, I overpaid and figured it out the next time I went there. It just so happened that the owner was present and so when I found out that there were different prices I just mentioned to him that the last time I was overcharged. Of course I did not have my receipt to prove that and I did not expect anything except to unburden my own failure to practice caveat emptorism (buyer beware). Even so, the owner gave me a pass for a free hour of racing. Naturally, when it came time to have my son's 5th year birthday party, I had such a sense of goodwill regarding that place, my husband and I decided to hold it there. We have been there at least a dozen times since then.

- The Good Egg purchased 3 tuna fish sandwiches for our bridge group from a fashionable gourmet food shop called Aux Delices. These sandwiches were not up to this shops usual snuff. Since it was my turn to treat for lunch, I went in to purchase three sandwiches, without the receipt, one week later. I asked to speak to the manager and in a pleasant and helpful manner I explained that the sandwiches were disappointing and we threw them out. The manager tried to figure out the problem, too many capers, or not enough/too much mayonnaise.

Finally she came back to me and stated that they had changed tuna fish vendors and thanked me for the feedback by giving me the three sandwiches I was about to purchase on the house. What I love about this story was that I did not even make the initial purchase and nevertheless was able to recover the wasted money.

- Did I tell you yet that I am a klutz? And who has not spilled a freshly delivered drink at a restaurant. My family and I did this three times at our recent vacation at the Westin in the Grand Cayman Island (a truly beautiful place). My husband was about to order a new drink, when I intervened and told the waitress that we had spilled our drink. All three times the spilled drinks were immediately replaced with the identical drink.

  If they had any doubts that we were in fact uncoordinated, one waitress witnessed a live occurrence. The savings was a little more than $20.00, a drop in the bucket of what we spent at this fabulous resort, but still why waste a penny if you do not have to? By the way I now officially call this maneuver the "Spilled Drink Do-Over".

- Sometimes you can get the most amazing things in return for your friendly feedback (complaints). When I was working I took my favorite clients to a restaurant in New York that The Good Egg raved about called D'Jango. The food was sublime however since it was fairly new the service was painfully slow. It was so slow that we had to miss dessert. I paid the bill and left, but as what often happens to me the regret sinks in later.

  Since I had left the scene and already paid the check, I knew that my only recourse was to call and be "helpful". I did just that, and to add a twist I did not ask for any money back. When I discussed the lunch with the manager and provided positive feedback along with some recommendations, she invited me back as her guest.

  Instead of accepting her generous invitation, I asked for a special party favor that they would give the guests who ordered champagne, a bistro chair made out the wire topping and wrapping of a champagne bottle. She readily agreed and had three of those charming bistro chairs made up for me that I gave to The Good Egg's daughters. My husband picked them up later that day on his way home.

By the way because this restaurant behaved so grandly I told my customer the story of the chairs. He loved the food and was impressed with their overwhelming graciousness that he now goes there frequently.

• When my family went to check in at the spectacular Broadmoor Hotel in Colorado Springs, our room was not ready. I asked if there was anything they could do to accommodate the inconvenience. I was swiftly handed vouchers for a round of free drinks.

What do all these stories have in common? It is that I was able to get discounts, refunds, coupons for free goods and "do-overs" by being reasonable, helpful and sometimes contrite. In some of these cases I did not even have receipts. I did not scream or carry-on, which sadly I sometimes do when it gets really brutal out there.

In a few cases such as AT&T Wireless and S&S Cleaners I fell on my sword and took the blame. I was reasonable and approached the situation as if I was providing valuable feedback in exchange for them correcting the situation. In other words it was "if I do this, will you do that".

You may ask what did they get? All of these businesses gained a loyal customer, and a customer who will sing their praises as often as I can. In addition, most of these transactions took place in front of other customers who got to witness their superb treatment of a valued customer.

But, what if I did not get the results that I wanted? In most of these examples, I might have dismissed these cases and blamed myself (or better yet my husband) for not being more careful in reading the receipts, waiting too long for recourse, making honest mistakes on my part (even tightwads occasionally let a nickel slip through).

In cases like this your best offense and defense is too throw yourself at the mercy of the court (those that hold the power to give you relief). If you do not get some compassion, you may think of doing business elsewhere in the future, because truly excellent businesses are interested in the relationship and will cut a customer some slack.

Do not forget either that this is a two way street! When you see that one of your precious merchants is in trouble you have to help them out (again, very you scratch my back and I will scratch yours). When Citibank misread a check I wrote to my honorary Saks Fifth Avenue and saved me oodles I money, I ran into Saks as soon as I could to make sure that they got the money they were entitled to. God forbid I underpay one of my hall of famers.

The best example ever regarding the give and take of the customer-vendor relationship was shown on an episode of "The Lucy Show". Lucy wanted to buy a new appliance that she could not afford. She shrewdly figured out a plot that revolved around returning baked beans that were having a "double your money back" offer if you were not satisfied. Lucy knew she could eventually be able to pay for her new washer/dryer if she kept doubling her money by buying, and then returning, cans of beans.

Lucy kept the scam up and would buy carts full of baked beans and return them, netting a tidy profit. Lucy's savvy scheme continued until the owner of the company that produced the baked beans noticed an uptick of returns and wanted to find out what was happening. He met up with Lucy and asked the vital question "Didn't you like the baked beans?"

Lucy had to admit that she had never tasted the baked beans, so she did right then and there. Well guess what, they were the best-baked beans she ever tasted. She could not continue the scheme once she realized how truly satisfying the baked beans were and returned all of the cans. In other words, the gig was up.

I cannot remember the ending if the owner bought her the appliance anyway. But it did not matter, when Lucy's integrity was tested, she could not continue to deceive the maker of this fabulous product or the store that she was bombarding with the returns. Ultimately Lucy did behave honorably and enjoyed those delectable baked beans for many years.

Rule: Make It Easy For The Other Party And Ask For What You Want

I love going to the movies. It is my big night out, so I hate it when anything goes wrong. Sometimes it does. Once I went to a movie that was listed in the paper and it was mysteriously cancelled. Another time, the theatre started the movie 30 minutes late. Once I even ordered tickets from Moviephone and arrived at the theatre only to find that it was closed.

What did I do? I asked for a free ticket. In each case I got a complimentary pass saving me $8.50 per shot. In the case of the Moviefone mishap I was actually given three tickets. It was certainly worth the 30 seconds it took for me to ask. But ask you must, and be specific. I did not just complain, I complained with a plan.

Here is my most embarrassing movie story. Once when I was playing hooky from my sales job in New York City I went to a matinee of this art house movie *Welcome to the Dollhouse*. There could not have been more than 15 minutes left when a mysterious person came in and dropped two huge duffle bags on seats in the middle of the theater. The other patrons starting looking around and gradually started to walk out. I did the same, fearing the worst. However, I was not in so much of a panic that on my way out I explained the situation to the manager and got two free tickets!

The end of this story is the next day I stopped by the theater to make sure everything was okay. Apparently they were having a preview for Disney's *Pocahontas* and the duffel bags were filled with little goodies for the children.

Rule: If You Used An Agent, Then Use Your Agent For The Refund!

If you conducted business through an agent whether a travel agent, a decorator or real estate agent use them to help do the negotiations for you. I was able to get a refund on a hideous hotel I stayed in with my husband in Budapest with the help of a travel agent.

This is what happened. Paul and I traveled to Eastern Europe before we got married. I booked the trip and trying to impress him with my sense of frugality (a virtue), I booked "value" hotels, more commonly known as really cheap ones.

Well, we suffered through our little place in Vienna (at least it was clean), but Paul put his foot down when we ended up at the Hotel Emke in Budapest. To give you an idea of how no-frills it was it used to be called the Hotel Karl Marx. The blankets did not even reach the foot of the bed. Calling it a fleabag would have been an insult to all the other dumpy hotels in the world.

I managed to gain credibility with Paul when I suggested we just leave the place and check into the Hilton on the other side of Budapest. When we left the Hotel Emke I asked if we could get some of our money back because it was so below what our expectations were. They refused.

I did not get too upset because in the back of my mind I knew that I was going to get my money back for the hotel later. When I returned home, I put a call into my travel agent and explained the situation. It took some time but I did receive a refund check for the days that were unused for more than $200.00.

Recently, I have engaged the help of my decorator to remedy a situation regarding my dining room set that she ordered for us. It has been trouble since the get go, but I drew the line when it starting squeaking so much when we ate I kept thinking that one of our cats was meowing. Anyway, I called and let her know how disappointed Paul and I were.

She is already on the case, and since she has placed many of these sets, had clout. She has just told me that the manufacturer will either fix or replace each piece that is not functioning properly. *News update!* The table and chair have been fixed at no cost and are no longer shaking and squeaking. I can start having dinner parties again.

Rule: Yes, You Can Negotiate With Doctors Too!

I can give you examples of several cases where I was able to get a refund for services rendered or billing that was questionable. When I was pregnant I had a hemorrhage and ended up hospitalized for 70 days in intensive care out of state. Luckily I wound up at Holy Cross Hospital in Silver Spring, Maryland and I truly believe I could not have received better care anywhere else. Plus I loved my Doctor, Dr. Richard Footer, whom I referred to as the "saint" or "beloved one". I must also add the nurses were "beyond the beyond" as my girlfriend Gail would say, or just simply divine.

My high-priced high risk Doctor in New York City when asked if it was okay to travel said it fine for me to do so. This was terrible medical advice for someone with my condition. In addition, the entire time I was hospitalized his office failed to send my records even after repeated calls from my Doctor, the nursing staff and me. Finally, after Matthew was born I nonchalantly brought up my Doctor in New York to the sainted Dr. Footer. It was then I found out that even after all of that effort the records never showed up.

Well, that is when steam came out of my ears. I called his fancy New York City office and demanded that they reimburse me for every cent I paid them. I said if I were litigious and if my Dad were not a Doctor (I have a very soft spot for Doctors), I would sue. Well, the same office that could not get it together enough to send out my file after 70 days worth of effort, sent out a check by certified mail that I received within 3 days.

My former Swiss boyfriend was one of the first persons I have known to have a type of lasik surgery. He was not at all happy with the results (this was over 10 years ago). He was not going to sue and I believe even signed a waiver because this procedure was so innovative. Anyway, he was disappointed with the results, even though he knew the risks that were involved. I suggested that he simply write the Doctor and say just that. Since he was so dissatisfied I also recommended that he ask for his money back. Within one week he received a check for the entire amount that he paid.

Just Ask At The Point Of Sale For A Discount

Generally I do not belabor this point, nor do I want to engage in a big haggling scene, but a simple "Can you do better"," or "Is there anything else you can do on the price" might get you some movement. I once received an immediate $50 discount when I said to the person restoring my furniture in my tiny little New York City apartment "Wow, that seems like a lot". I refer to this maneuver officially as "asking for the nice person's discount".

The best practical example of this technique that I can give you was at a rug store. I went shopping with my husband and we picked out two Oriental rugs. Once we knew what we wanted we piled them up and then I simply asked if we could get an additional discount. I need to take a break from this story and point out that when I say "we", I really mean "me". Within five minutes the manager came back and said we could take off $400.00. Of course this works best with small businesses and when you are dealing directly with the owner.

It also works best when you are traveling abroad in countries that expect you to bargain. Even though I make it a point not to shop when I travel, I so enjoyed the wrangle my friend Marion and I were having somewhere in the sub Sahara that I got carried away. The next thing I knew I was into an intense haggle with one of those gorgeous Omar Shariff looking Blue People. I ended up with a fabulous little rug for $100.00 that I love.

I also found myself doing this in Cuzco, Peru over a sweater, my only purchase in what could be considered a shopping paradise. In those places it is really part of the buying process. In America, it is not standard, but it can work, so it can pay off to simply ask. Remember, nothing ventured, nothing gained.

I Guess The Entire World Is Getting Better Rates At Hotels

The New York Times Business Section on Sunday March 9, 2003 had a section on how people are putting in much more effort in trying to get lower hotel rates. Basically this article advises asking for additional discounts or packages and comparing rates quoted on sites such as Expedia.com. When you call the hotel directly to book your trip have the lower rates that you found ready, so they know what price point you are looking for.

This article also recommends calling frequently, especially close to the date of your arrival and ask for better rates. In addition, negotiations are most successful with large chains, which have better tracking information and may try harder to accommodate a loyal customer. Another worthwhile suggestion was to make sure to check to see if you get a discount if you belong to an association such as AAA or AARP.

Need a hotel for a few hours between a layover or need to extend your trip for a few hours? Most hotels offer a day rate, a little known fact, but if you ask for it you may get a room for almost one-third less than the regular rate. You usually need to be out by 6 or 7 pm, but it certainly beats paying full price for something you will not be using up.

You Can Negotiate With Bundles Better!

This reminds me of that saying "Cheaper by the dozen". In other words, sometimes when you are buying something, and they will not give you a discount, add an extra smaller item and see if that will get them to budge. My friend told me that he did this when buying a big-screen television. He asked for a little something off. They said "no". He then asked if he was to add on a small little one for the kitchen would they reconsider. They gave him the second television for half price.

I also make sure I buy package deals when the discount gets larger the more you buy. I buy my exercise classes in the largest bucket available so that it drives the cost per class down.

What To Do If All Fails And You Are Stuck With A Loser

Tag-sale if you can—I know in my community it is easy to do, but some towns are not so accommodating. If this is your situation, have it at friends in a tag-sale friendly place. I have been saving up my "candidates for resale" for the past year. I have set-up a staging area in my basement where I put things once they are considered tag-sale worthy.

Not only can you make some decent money (at my first tag-sale I made $900), but also they are really fun. It is fascinating to see what people buy. The best part happens before the first customer arrives and you can swap stuff with your friends. My friends and I were surprised with how much stuff we swapped between ourselves before we opened to the general public.

Rule: Getting A Tax-Deduction Is Better Than Nothing

This is another "when all else fails category". What if you cannot return it, tag sale it or negotiate in anyway with the stores, if you cannot go to small claims court or the Attorney General? Let's just say you are with an object that you just cannot look at because it represents so much disappointment. First ask if it has anything redeeming. If so, and someone else might be able to wear it, or use it, bring it to The Good Will or the Salvation Army and take that tax-deduction. Do not forget to save that receipt and file it immediately so you do not misplace it.

9

The Art Of Escalation—Getting Ugly!

Rule: When Honey Does Not Work Resort To Vinegar (Better Known As The Squeaky Wheel Syndrome)

We have covered many tactics that you can use in order to rescue money that dangles over the great cash wasteland. But once in awhile something falls through the cracks, and sadly and surprisingly your sweetness, promptness and receipts are not doing the job.

There are many options before you should get ugly—but now we have to face reality. They will sadly not always work. Now is the time to figure out what to do next after you have exhausted all the pleasant options. To put it bluntly we are going to cover what to do when the honey was just making a big sticky mess and you are stuck in it. You have failed to make lemons out of lemonade. In other words, you need the vinegar.

Warning! The faint of heart can stop reading right now and skip to the next chapter because this is when and where the proverbial "rubber hits the road", or "the @#(*& hits the fan" or when "the boys are separated from the men."

I realize that I am going to lose some readers here. Some people just do not like a good fight, and would rather live in a state of blissful peace. For them it is just easier to forget about the money. My husband would say at this critical point "Life is too short." I do not like to fight, but if I am feeling self-righteous I will put up a great one. This is precisely when I would ask myself "Am I a woman, or am I a mouse?"

But what if you have done what I recommended and find yourself up against a brick wall? What if you have been a wise shopper and saved your receipts, if you were timely in returning your merchandise and were adequately pleasant in your attempt to be satisfied with your transaction, and all of this fails? It can happen and it has happened to me. If you find yourself in this situation, I recommend the following steps in the order presented. In all of my adventures in money rescuing they have never failed me.

Ask For An Even Exchange Or Store Credit

I know, I know. I do not usually like to get a store credit or an even exchange; I prefer to get my money back or a credit on my charge card. However, it is often easier for a merchant to give you this, so if you are getting nowhere with a refund, ask to get something of equal value or a credit. It is better than nothing, and surely you can find one more thing that you like in the store.

It Is Better To Have A Fight In Person

It is much easier to get your way, if you show up in person to have your squabble. First off, they take on the risk of alienating customers by creating a scene. You in turn, lower your risk of really going cuckoo-coconuts and ending up with scorched earth rather than a refund.

Case in point, I have recently been in the throws of attempting to get a proper bill from a Doctor's office so that I can get reimbursed from my insurance company. After many phones calls I still did not receive a correct bill. Finally, I could not stand the runaround anymore so I just popped in the office. Only then did I get a bill that had the correct information so that I could collect the 80% my insurance covered.

What if I did not make that "friendly" little visit? I could have kept calling to no avail. Or I could have done what many others (including my husband) would have done after so much irritation, and just given up.

By waiting around for the Doctor's office to eventually come through with the goods, I could have missed the deadline my insurance company gave me to rectify the situation. They did not take me seriously until I was looking them straight in the eyes. I saved $140.00 by simply showing up, and I hate to say this because it sounds so "in your face," but I had to get in their face.

Stay On Top Of It

This is basically more of the same on how you need to pro-actively manage the situation, not by just keeping your documents organized and checking what has been resolved, but by following-up and calling and visiting. In other words, you need to manage (bug) them until you reach the resolution that you can live with.

Sometimes I wonder if many businesses are set up to function this way deliberately because they know how hard it is for most people to keep on a "case." Perhaps they know the many reasons that the customers drop these issues. I can name a few: the customer is too, busy, timid, disorganized, sees the process as too much of a hassle, and has other distractions. Sometime the reason is just plain ignorance and the customer may not even be aware that there is recourse or that they have any rights.

I cannot tell you how many times I have had to fight these things round after round until the situation was settled. Here is an example. I went to my local bank and tried to get $100.00 out of the ATM. I got a receipt for the withdrawal but no cash. I picked up the phone that was located by the machine and immediately reported it.

I was told to wait two days for them to reconcile all of the transactions. It seems pretty easy doesn't it? They look at deposits and withdrawals and count the cash on hand. Still, I waited two days. Then I called. Then I was told to wait a month. Nothing happened.

This is the point in time where I can imagine that somewhere in my bank there is a person who looks like Snidely Whiplash saying "Yippee we lost that one, tee-hee another $100.00 for us". Well I had to stay on them for weeks, calling almost every day. I escalated and I spoke to people all over the bank. I did eventually get my money back, but I just could not wait for them to get around to it. Mainly because it appeared as if that day would never come.

Escalate To The Manager, Or Owner Of The Store, Retell Your Story, And Show The Receipts

What happens if you cannot return things by using the techniques I have reviewed? Let's say you go in with a receipt, within a reasonable period of time (a month) and the item is defective. To add insult to injury you are even sweeter and friendlier than what is natural for your disposition. What if you do not get your item refunded? Here are the next steps. First, escalate, by asking to see the store manager.

- Start out by stating the following, that you are sure they want you to be satisfied and want your repeat business. Please do not forget to say the magic word "satisfied". I have a hunch that the importance of customer satisfaction is plastered all over the lunchrooms in most stores. This is where it is key that you have an established relationship.

• If they will not give you a refund, ask for a store credit, or preferably an item of the same value also known as an even exchange.

It is rare for your case to not be resolved at this point. My girlfriend Donna was in a store once and this reasonable woman with a receipt was trying to return merchandise. The manager and sales persons were so inflexible and snotty to the poor returnee that my girlfriend decided she did not want to shop in that store and left.

By the way, Donna is a platinum level shopper at Saks so they missed out on a great future customer. Stores ought to know that customers want a pleasant shopping experience soup to nuts and ought not want to turn them off with a distasteful scene.

I would like to share a story of how I was able to return a Ferragamo bag that I bought at Bloomingdales almost one year after I purchased it. After a year most people would not bother. For those of you who had the pleasure of owning any Ferragamo product you know that the quality is outstanding.

That was the essential point of my argument. This is how the transaction started. I first went to the sales lady in the handbag department. When she refused to take it back, I asked to see her manager, and he also would not budge. Then I asked to see the Divisional Manager. His first line of defense was "Lady that bag is almost a year old". He relented when I used the following line of logic. I replied with "for the price of that bag I expected to get more than 10 months out of it before it fell apart". Within 10 minutes I walked out of Bloomingdales with a stunning Palomo Picasso bag that I adored and wore for years.

Turn On The Heat By Calling Headquarters

If the answer is still "no" continue going up the food chain until you speak to the owner or highest ranking manager on the premises. If that option is exhausted call the owner/president's office in the home office. If you have a cell phone why not do it on their premises, I bet that would irk them.

Once I had a fight at a store that is now out of business regarding a "cutless coupon." That is how they referred to a coupon that was sent in one of those packages of coupons that you receive in the mail. It was for $100.00 off a pool table.

When my husband went to buy the pool table the salesperson explained to him that the price marked on the table already included the coupon price. So my husband came home with the order and no additional discount reflecting the coupon I made him carry in. That just did not wash with me, so I went to the store and was given the same load of garbage. I admit it, I had a fight with the manager right on the premises. I am sure other shoppers were turned off.

I left with my "cutless coupon" and called the home office and I spoke with "Bob" the owner. He reiterated the whole cutless coupon when I pulled my strategic advantage that it was a "bait and switch", which is considered false advertising. I then added that I was going to report this situation to the Attorney General's Office. Well within a few minutes I received a certificate via fax for $100 worth of merchandise. Naturally I redeemed this immediately since I suspected a store that operated this way would go out of business. It did.

Remember my hospital story. Well I kept myself busy one day when I received a bouquet of flowers that was shockingly unappealing. To be fair and to make sure my criticism was not due to the lack of sleep that one experiences while hospitalized, I consulted with the nurses. They all agreed it was the most ugly flower arrangement that they had ever seen, and nurses in big hospitals have seen it all!

First I called the florist and complained that the arrangement was unacceptable, and I wanted it replaced. They said they disagreed and that there was nothing they would do. Now I was in a pickle. I wanted to escalate but I did not know who to do that to since this was a small local florist. In addition, I did not want to seem ungrateful to my friends that sent it, nor did I want them to feel bad. Therefore I refrained from calling them to get more information.

I took a shot and called 1-800-flowers, hoping since this was sent from my friends in New York that this would be the service they would use. When I explained the situation, they were able to trace the delivery because the florist was a member.

Within 24 hours I had an improved bouquet. Even though it still was not up to par with some of the other magnificent bouquets I received, I was, however, happy with the replacement.

Did you also know that if you receive roses from a florist and they do not open fully, you usually can get them replaced? For the price of a dozen, you should expect roses to bloom and last for one week. So if this happens to you and your roses flop rather than bloom call and ask for a substitute. I have a great florist in Cos Cob, and on the rare occasion when I am treated to roses, I have had them last for eight to nine days.

I also want to tell about my mother's theory about florists. Whenever she sends flowers out of town she always makes a point to say she will be seeing the flowers when she visits the recipient. She is convinced that florists will send inferior arrangements to someone if the sender will never be able to check the quality.

There is one more example that I would like to share with you on how going to the top paid off and saved me from having a severe anxiety attack. I was traveling in Kenya and went to the airport for my departing flight only to find a painfully long and slow line. My flight was leaving at midnight and by 11:30 I still had not checked in. Right when I was going to step up to the counter, someone cut right in front of me.

Well I was incensed that after such an exhausting wait someone would just dash in and take my place in line. Naturally I was irritated. Anyway I started tapping him on the back and kept repeating, "Excuse me" in an indignant tone of voice. Finally the perpetrator turned around and I recognized him right away. He was world famous.

I will shorten this story by saying I did not get on the flight even though I had a valid ticket. As a matter of fact I had to take a public bus back to my hotel in Nairobi late at night. Luckily I got my room back.

The next morning I went to the tour operator and they confirmed a spot for me on a morning flight. I went to the airport again and sure enough I could not get back on. I should add that the same crew who worked the desk the prior night was back. They remembered that it did not go well when they made me miss my first flight.

To make matters worse the ticket counter personnel informed me that all the flights were booked. Needless to say I was hysterical. My only hope was to find someone with authority who worked for the airline who would help me. I dragged my suitcase across the airport to the executive offices. I went straight to the president's door and asked his secretary if I could see him. I waited and waited but finally he allowed me a brief visit.

When he heard my story he was extremely distressed by how I was treated. After a short inquiry he discovered that I could have been on all the flights. He then requested that the manager on duty carry back my luggage and get me on the next flight. He went so far as to make sure there was someone waiting to greet me in Frankfurt and to make sure I was able to get my connecting flight. The airline even paid for my overnight accommodations in Germany.

I must say I was really touched by his decency. I also need to add that even though my trip ended on a somewhat sour note, I thought that Africa, and its amazing wildlife, was one of the most beautiful and most interesting places I have ever visited.

Call Your Credit Card Company Immediately If You Charged The Items Or Services In Jeopardy And File A Dispute As Soon As Possible

American Express is undoubtedly the best at this. I had a lovely friend Ed Rogoff (Ed if you are reading this I am sorry we fell so out of touch) who bought an electronic item that failed to operate properly. After haggling with the store and not getting any recourse there (I am sure he never set foot in that establishment again), Ed was exasperated. We brainstormed and decided that the easiest and fastest way was to file a dispute against the merchant with American Express. Luckily, Ed got his money back, and I got a free lunch as a thank you from Ed.

The irony here is that when we went to order lunch I ordered a ham and cheese sandwich with pickles. Instead I got a ham and cheese with pesto. I did not return it because Ed was so happy that he "won" the dispute that I did not want to cast any spell of unpleasantness on the occasion. Of course, I still regret that I did not just take the sandwich back and get the correct version. I just toss this up as the return that got away.

But before I digress on the details of how easy this can be, please try this as your second attempt for recourse after you have gone all the way up the organization. Credit Cards are more vested in protecting the consumer than the merchant.

File A Report With The Attorney Generals Office

This is pretty easy to do but it is a very slow process. The best part is that it is free so you do not risk any outlays of cash while you try to collect. In other words, you are not going to throw any more good money after bad. In addition, it is a major pain in the neck for any merchant and casts an ugly, ugly curse over them. My experience has taught me that this is an excellent "motivator."

While I have never seen this through from start to finish, I have threatened this twice, with the pool table store, and the agent selling my wonderful tiny condominium in New York City during the height of the real estate hysteria in the 1980's (where I sadly won the condominium in a bidding war only to grossly overpay). In both cases just the sheer ugliness of the threat was enough to motivate them to rectify the situation.

You will have to fill out some forms, but all States have this service and it is a low cost source of restitution. I recently was able to fill out a report for the State of New York that was located on the Attorney Generals Office website. This was time efficient and saved me the cost of the stamp to file it. Incidentally, I later decided to drop the case, once the merchant and I cleared up the misunderstanding.

Go To Small Claims Court

I actually have used this twice and have won both times. It is a low cost method (it costs around $30.00) of recouping your loses and the threat of it does create a major pain for the merchant. However, in both cases it did go the whole 9 yards, so if you are serious you may find yourself sitting around your local courthouse. In addition, there is a dollar limit on the awards for claims. The threat of the suit with the tiresome paperwork and the pending court date did not deter either a huge travel agency or a small now defunct plumbing company.

First let me explain what the problem was with both situations and what prompted me to take both of these cases to court. When I was in my early twenties I took a trip to the Canary Islands with my brother Paul. I found the trip in the Sunday paper in an advertisement that stated it included deluxe accommodations.

When my brother and I arrived we were horrified at the state of our hotel. To help you conjure up an image of how bad it was keep in mind that we were still in our early twenties with very low standards. I had recently backpacked through Europe on $10 a day and was never as badly offended. Many of the other travelers in our tour group left and found "deluxe" accommodations but my brother and I stuck it out in the red light district.

When I returned home I immediately called the agency that booked the trip. After months of getting the run around and arguing over the meaning of "deluxe" I was advised by my friend the lawyer to go to small claims court.

I was actually surprised that they did not want to settle and I had to go to court. It was even more shocking that they hired a lawyer over a case worth $1058.00. But nonetheless there I was telling my sad story to the judge. I had the advertisement in hand since the travel agency was still trying to lure unsuspecting tourist to this dreadful destination.

I really did not know which way this case was going to go until the lawyer for the defendant said as a summation, "What does she expect for $529.00 per person?" With that the judge said she expected what you promised—deluxe accommodations. We settled for $750.00.

The plumbing company is an even bleaker story. When I arrived home after being hospitalized out of town for 70 days with a preemie I did not need to get saddled with a massive plumbing problem. But one evening during the summer of 1997 my husband went to turn on the water and only droplets came out. To make a monotonous story bearable, in our rush to fix the problem we hired one of the few local plumbers who could have handled such a large job to try to find the leak.

Of course, it would have been much easier and cheaper if our water company just fixed it. But they determined that the problem was ours because the curb box was so far off our property and the connection to the main was originally on a private street. In other words they were completely off the hook. Even after my dramatic appeal when I showed up at the President's office in my demure little flowered chemise with the baby in his little basket, they still refused to help.

I will just say now that it cost us over $50,000 to fix the problem and to return water to our home. Insurance picked up $13,000 which covered some landscaping and a new septic tank to replace what the backhoe crushed.

When we went to sell the house a year later we learned that the owner, a licensed plumber did not get permits for his work and left out a crucial component, baffles. Had we not had the house inspected who knows what damage might have been caused by his substandard work. The cost to remedy the situation and have it pass the Department of Health standards was over $1600.00. The owner did not respond to any of my requests for him to fix the situation.

As a matter of fact he did not return my calls when I called him for assistance. What was even more annoying was that I knew he was there. I would ask if he was there. First they would say, "yes" until they found out who it was and then he would suddenly disappear. I know this has had to happen to you at least once in your life. Isn't it infuriating?

Considering I allowed the plumbers in and out of my home, served them lemonade and paid in full promptly you would think they would show a little consideration. I even lent them a copy of the videotape (which was never returned) from the local news report on our story.

After being given the major blow off by the owner, and after a reputable plumber resolved everything, I took the awful (and not defunct) plumbing company to court. He never showed up and the judge even wondered after hearing the case why I sued for only $1600.00 rather than the entire amount.

In the end, it did not matter that I won, or what I won because he never paid his judgment. In order to maintain his license he had to pay within six months. What I finally received was a notice that he declared bankruptcy and informed me that I was not allowed to harass him. I later joked that if I could not have the money I was awarded or the joy of harassing him, what was the point?

What did I do next? Later you will learn the stunning conclusion when I suggest another option, going directly to the state licensing board for licensed professionals. And of course even though I won both cases, there is the collection problem to deal with that is why one of my mottos is "suing is over-rated".

Why "Sue The Bastards" Isn't As Much Fun As It Sounds

Let's face it, it can be flat out fun to threaten to sue someone, but in reality more times than not you end up getting screwed more than the person you plan to sue. I will explain this to you with a true story that happened to me on my 28th birthday.

I was at a deck party at my friend's rental house in Westport, Connecticut. My fiancée at the time, Bob said that he was worried that the deck would not be able to hold all the people jumping and dancing, as well as the heavy bar that was plopped on it. When there were over 40 people and Bob said again that this was making him nervous, I just rolled my eyes and called him a weenie (or something worse).

No sooner than my insult left my lips then the deck swung out from under my feet and I fell, along with all the other guests into a big heap 16 feet below. It was a miracle that no one got seriously hurt, but there were some broken bones. I had some cuts and bruises, but after a tetanus shot and a week or two, my cuts healed and I was fine.

Not so with Bob, who broke his foot when I allegedly landed on it. But more than just his foot was wounded. Bob just could not get over the negligence of the builder. He wanted more than just the compensation for his injuries; he wanted the homeowners to be found guilty of negligence.

Within two weeks of this accident, I was contacted by the insurance company and asked to settle for $1500.00. I called my friend the lawyer and he said basically that there is a rate card and that since I had no permanent injuries, to take the money and walk. I did. The insurance representative also told me that Bob would be given $20,000 to settle now. Bob refused this offer. So did half a dozen others who decided to gamble on a class action lawsuit.

I will jump ahead five years later. During those five years Bob and the others had dreams of new cars, new boats, expensive trips all paid for with the huge windfall from the pending lawsuit. What they got was exactly what was offered initially (right off the chart) less the 33% for the lawyer's fee. Plus they had to wait five years, meaning that inflation eroded some of the value of the money they won.

They also lost out on the potential income they could have made by investing that money during that time, or the benefit of having that money now rather than later. The lesson here is that in many cases you are better off working directly with the insurance company or whoever your "defendant" is for compensation.

Here is a story of how I refrained from filing a frivolous lawsuit and instead worked directly with the business to achieve desirable results. A few months ago when I went on vacation to a resort I broke my front tooth on a turkey club sandwich. This was a pretty glamorous place and instead of looking just like the normal mess I am when I travel, I looked like Ellie May from *The Beverly Hillbillies*. I was so bummed out.

Of course my husband thought it was no big deal and the kids found it fascinating. But I must say, I was extremely self-conscious and was upset over the whole matter. So this is what I did. I called the General Manager's office and explained the situation. Then I called my dentist in New York City and asked for his guidance. He suggested I go to a dentist down there and get a temporary cap. I did that. When I returned home I saw my dentist and he replaced my tooth. It looks as good as new.

The hotel not only graciously bought me a free Bahama Mama to ease my pain (it helped), but also paid for all of my expenses associated with the unfortunate incident. Did I have to go through the pain and drudgery of a lawsuit? No way, I got reimbursed for everything two months later. Best of all everyone was so civilized and kind that the entire episode in no way ruined what was otherwise a terrific trip.

But that is not my only caution as to why you should think twice before you go sue-crazy. I have come to notice a pattern with lawyers, be it divorce, employment or personal injury. I call it the "Big Tease". This is what happens; you go in with your sad story. You pay "The Retainer" (this is also known as the sacrificial lamb). The lawyer talks it up big, the big bucks you are gonna get, how he/she is gonna get them. God forbid you ever go and spend this money before your chickens hatch!!

Now that you are enjoying the fantasy of the big outrageous award that will make the papers and teach that #(@*$&@ a lesson, all of a sudden your lawyer drops the bomb. Your case is not so good. They never actually say that but this is the time when you start to hear about your risks or why your case is weak.

Guess what also, between your first visit and this eye-opener visit you have depleted "The Retainer". You also may have lost any goodwill with the person/entity you were going to teach a lesson to so you can no longer try to negotiate or win them over with honey.

I ask you to check my "Big Tease" theory out. Two of my friends just learned this when they were laid off and went to an employment lawyer. They were all pumped up after the first meeting only to be given the bitter truth weeks or months later. I was anticipating that they would get the "Big Tease". They did.

Really, try not to sue to resolve your problems. This should be the absolute last resort especially if you have to pay "The Retainer". In my own experience and those of my family and friends, you just add more pain to your bad experience, and of course you have thrown away more money (better known as "The Retainer"!)

Does The Better Business Bureau Really Matter?

No. I have tossed this one around with everybody's most wanted enemy, a contractor, with no avail. A long time ago I even wrote the Better Business Bureau a letter regarding a dry cleaner, which stored my fur coat in plastic (that was before I became a Peta convert, now I buy down jackets and wash them myself for free).

But in all cases, this gets the smallest rise from my antagonist. I think I know why. Did you ever meet a consumer who consulted with the Better Business Bureau before hiring a contractor or going to a merchant? Neither have I. Most cases are only left on the records for a year which only dilutes the potential punch you are trying to swing that much more. So I consider this the least effective method for recourse, but you can try and see if you get a reaction. Please let me know if you do.

The Surprise Of The Licensing Organization

To get to the licensing bureau of the professional you wish to make a complaint against, called your State's Department of Consumer Protection. I have done this twice, once for a Psychiatrist who was stretching the boundaries on his billing practices and the other on a plumbing company, after I won a judgment but could not collect because the owner filed for bankruptcy.

The only case I took to a licensing board was the "evil" plumber. I am sure the owner never thought that I would drive over one and one half hours to Hartford to attend a hearing. He never even showed up to defend himself. There was a 40 minute hearing whereupon an investigator found him to be "unethical" not only in his practices but in his work standards.

In addition as a licensed plumber you are required to pay all judgments with in a certain time frame, which we all know he failed to do. The conclusion was that he lost his license and I felt rewarded that he would not be out taking advantage of other consumers by grossly overcharging and underperforming.

Call The Police

Of course this seems drastic and it is. But it has worked for two of my friends who were in binds. First was "Martha" and her decorator. "Martha" gave her decorator $5000 for fabric. Over one year later the decorator produced nothing and "Martha" asked for her money back. She did not get it.

Her husband hired a lawyer who wrote a few letters (probably just enough to use up "The Retainer"). Again, nothing happened. When "Martha" told me her story I said "enough was enough" and suggested she just call the police. After all, when you are dealing with that kind of money, it is considered grand larceny.

Well, "Martha" was smart and called the decorator first. She preferred getting the money back to putting the decorator in prison. Within 24 hours of her no nonsense call "Martha" had cashed the check and recovered the money. I was treated to a vente white chocolate frappucino at Starbucks for my astute advice.

I have to leave names and details out, but one of my girlfriends who owns a small business was given two consecutive bad checks from the same customer. It was for thousands of dollars. After getting the run around for weeks she finally threatened to call the police. A charge card was given (sadly by a family member who had to cover for the dead beat) and she was able to collect. I do believe in both cases this was the only alternative, besides simply accepting the financial loss.

Final Farewell

I have to be honest; I have given almost all I have to give so this is going to be a very lackluster finale. I am going to attempt to rally because you paid good money for this book, or at the very least paid a little bit for it at a tag sale. Even if you paid nothing and got my masterpiece at the library, you most likely had to drive there, so you should get a decent ending. Remember, I am on your side.

So, now I wish you the best and will send you off to the real world with your coupons in hand and chutzpah in your heart. Remember to avoid spending at all if you can, but if you do, buy only what you love. If you find that you did waste some money (and it happens to us all), refer to my tips to rescue that money and give it a second chance to perform.

Do not forget that your nest egg is your ticket to freedom, so nurture it as a mother hen would her little baby (the egg). Be nice to your merchants and play fair so they will be inclined to treat you well and give you some slack when you need it. And for goodness sake while you managing all this do not do any of this at the risk of being stingy.

Be mindful that it is great to have financial security and to be savvy with money, but is more important to be a good person. Or as Bob Hope used to say, "it is nice to be important, but it is more important to be nice". (By the way I am unsure if he did actually say that but what the heck, let's say he did. Plus it is so sweet I doubt he would have been mad if I did not attribute it properly. Frankly, I wouldn't care if someone said I said that! If he never said it and it is an unclaimed quote, then I will take it as mine!)

Now, after we take the Forever Frugal pledge I will bid farewell to my wise and lovely readers!

"I swear that before I spend anything I will pay myself first. I will build my nest egg like the tortoise and care for it like the mother hen nurtures the chick. I will from now on think long and hard before I spend my hard earned money. I will not waste what was earned through my earnest labor. I will rescue all that was squandered. I will attempt many remedies before I ever give up on recovering my wasted funds. And most importantly, when I have my "F YOU MONEY" I will still be as nice as I was when I was accumulating it".

Congratulations, you have completed your lesson. But before we part I want to give you one last tip. Why not track the money that you have rescued through-out the year. I do this weekly. It is fun and rewarding to see how much you have saved from your smart money management. But remember no splurging unless you have been diligent in fattening that nest egg. And now I bid you a fond fare-well!

0-595-31292-6

Printed in the United States
97788LV00002B/184/A

9 780595 312924